BALES
&
BANKS

Of bales and banking

Growing up in 1950s rural England

Mike Pitcher

Of bales and banking
Growing up in 1950s rural England
Mike Pitcher

Illustrations Raphelina Bonito

ISBN 978 1 909660 21 2
A CIP catalogue record for this book is available from the British Library.

Published 2013 by Tricorn Books
www.tricornbooks.co.uk
131 High Street
Portsmouth
PO1 2HW

Tricorn Books

Printed & bound in UK

Illustrations
Raphelina Bonito

For my grandchildren:
Olivia, Annabel, Emilia, Toby
and any others to come, so that they may know
I wasn't always rich, famous and handsome.
(Well, I was always handsome of course).

Contents

Page

An introductory explanation 1

Essential preliminary reading 3

Chapter 1: What to do? 7

Chapter 2: Learning the game 21

Chapter 3: It's so easy 37

Chapter 4: Everyday 55

Chapter 5: Look at me 69

Chapter 6: It's not my fault 85

Chapter 7: Soft place in my heart 101

Chapter 8: Reminiscing 115

Chapter 9: Heartbeat 129

Thanks 147

For any comments or enquiries regarding this book please contact: *michaelpitcher@outlook.com*

An introductory explanation

Earlier this year I mentioned to my sons that at the age of seventy, I was giving up paid work after fifty-three years. Or perhaps it was giving up on me?

My eldest lad, knowing how fidgety I can become with idle hands, suggested I should write my memoirs.

On first hearing, I dismissed this notion out of hand. However, the thought grew in my head that I ought at least to jot down some recollections about my early years for the benefit of my grandchildren. I had read somewhere that around 40% of all grandchildren know nothing about their grandparents. That seemed a great shame, so about a month after the first conversation I had produced an early draft of what I hope you are about to enjoy.

For many years I have been a devotee of Alfred Wainwright, the poor boy from very humble origins in Blackburn, who became justifiably famous for his unique pictorial guides to the English Lake District. In some personal reflections at the end of his final volume he describes his books as love letters to the fells.

For me what follows is also a letter of love and gratitude. I am one of the luckiest people alive and my good fortune started with an immensely happy and wonderfully golden childhood. Indeed, it was so good that I decided some time ago to relinquish any attempt at adulthood and stay a child forever!

I shall follow A.W.'s example in donating any profits from this book to charity. As ever, he put it so aptly when he wrote:

"One surely does not wish to be paid for writing a love-letter!"

Mike Pitcher, Hong Kong and Guernsey, September 2013

Essential preliminary reading

1. The Wiltshire Moonraker Legend

There was a time when smuggling was a significant industry in rural England, with Wiltshire providing an important staging post between suppliers on the south coast and customers in the country's heartland.

The story goes that one bright moonlit night in the late eighteenth century, a band of smugglers based in Devizes, an old market town in the centre of the county, had hidden barrels of contraband French brandy in the Crammer pond by the town green. At dead of night whilst beginning to retrieve their loot with long hay rakes, the smugglers were suddenly confronted by excise men who had been tipped off that something was afoot in the vicinity of St James' Church.

Surrounded by the government revenue men demanding an explanation of what they were doing, the leader of the gang quick as a flash pointed at the moon's reflection on the water and explained they were "raking out thet gurt, round, yeller cheese in yonder pool."

The excise people relaxed and broke into smiles. Clearly these country yokels were simpletons to believe such a ridiculous story. Satisfied they had just encountered a bunch of fools attempting to rake in the reflection of the moon, imagining it to be a giant cheese, the government men mounted up and rode off chuckling to themselves as they went.

The 'village idiots' had the last laugh as they later hauled in the numerous barrels of fine brandy. They drank a little to celebrate their success and despatched the remainder northwards to their thirsty clients.

To this day people born and raised in Wiltshire are proud to call themselves Moonrakers.

2. Extract from 'Moondreams' by Buddy Holly

> "*Strange things take place in my moondreams*
> *As the lonely and loveless hours go by*
> *Your face takes its place in every moonbeam*
> *Moondreams bring thoughts gentle as a sigh*."

Composed by Norman Petty, Manager and Producer of Buddy Holly and The Crickets (1957 – 8). Recorded by Buddy Holly with the Dick Jacobs Orchestra at Coral Record Studios, New York, on the 21st of October 1958. The recording became a posthumous release as the flip side of the much better known 'True Love Ways' in 1960. This last session produced Buddy's only recordings with strings, a novelty for a rock artist in its day.

Chapter 1: What to do?

"Made your mind up yet, Pitcher?"

Was the kindly and concerned enquiry from Lump Lewis, who trebled as senior maths teacher, careers master and deputy head at Devizes Grammar School. To this day, no-one recalls what he might have done to deserve his strange nickname.

"Not yet sir, nothing appeals," came the unsurprising reply. We had trodden this path together a few times before.

"Come and meet me in the careers room after school today and we'll see if we can make some progress. Time and tide," he encouraged, "time and tide..."

Lump was typical of the schoolteachers of that era. He had been at the school for half its existence and stayed there until the day he retired. He was gentle yet firm, humorous but deadly serious when the need arose, always ready to encourage maths strugglers but equally fast to admonish those who were slipping behind through laziness. To use a phrase which sadly no longer seems fashionable, he set an example. Of course, we pupils were also different from many of those today; sorry, my lovely grandchildren, but we were. Although we got up to all sorts of pranks, it all amounted to pretty harmless stuff. We respected our parents, we admired our teachers and we were ardently loyal to our school.

Even the 1955 film *Blackboard Jungle* with its unbelievable scenes of classroom mayhem in the United States didn't shake our established views. The film shocked us, it became a must-see after originally being refused a certificate by the British Board of Film Censors, but it was all happening on a different planet to the one we were inhabiting.

However, one aspect of the film did change the lives of some of us. The theme music was 'Rock Around the Clock' by Bill Haley and the Comets. The sound, the beat, the rhythm; it was like nothing we had ever encountered before. In some cinemas, on first release, the tune was not broadcast at all because the style was considered such a bad influence. One critic of the day described it as a fourth-rate film with fifth-rate music, but acknowledged the beat could "turn youngsters into wild dervishes."

I made a guitar during woodwork class because I wanted to play and sing like Haley. I just stopped short of copying his kiss curl. The guitar was rubbish and my singing was worse, so I formed a three-man skiffle group, which was the other big musical fad of the day. Who could fail to be moved by the king of the genre Lonnie Donegan's hit of the moment 'Diggin' My Potatoes'? None of us had any money, of course, so one played a big bass made from a tea-chest, broom-handle and a piece of string, whilst the other 'borrowed' his mother's washboard which was played using metal thimbles on the fingers and thumbs. You will discover in a moment why I would have been even more useless on this particular musical instrument. I was self-appointed vocalist and acoustic (please don't look too closely) guitarist.

We auditioned to play at the annual senior school party. The judges were three teachers: Lump, Miss R and Killer Howells. I can't remember what Miss R taught but she was gorgeous. Every male student over the age of fifteen was in love with her, and most under the age of fifteen pretended they were.

Killer was the music teacher. His nickname was not chosen at random. We got halfway through 'Rock Island Line' when he could contain himself no longer.

"Pitcher, that's not skiffle – it's piffle! Get out!" he roared. "And don't come back," he added somewhat unnecessarily.

My mate's mum was pleased to get her washboard back. Skiffle went out of fashion nationwide shortly thereafter. I fear I may have played a small part in its demise.

It was, however, a great style of music to get amateurs going, and one of the many skiffle groups to be formed during this period was The Quarrymen, started in March 1957 by a certain John Winston Lennon, when he was only sixteen. Perhaps if I had bought myself a decent guitar?

There were no illegal drugs in Moonraker country in those days; indeed, we wouldn't have known what the phrase meant. But as several people have remembered since, we got high on Rock 'n Roll. It still sends shivers down my spine.

When I first started at the grammar school in 1953 I was like a fish out of water for the first year. I had been the king of a very small domain in my village, leader of the pack, but here I was a nobody. Most of the pupils had known each other for many years, having previously attended other schools in Devizes. One somewhat biased glance told me they were middle-class townies who were looking down their snooty noses at the likes of me. In fairness, my thick rural accent and country-boy demeanour probably created a barrier which was difficult for them to cross initially as well, even if they had wanted to.

“that’s not skiffle - it’s piffle!”

EXIT
AUDITIONS
FOR
SCHOOL
CONCERT
TONIGHT
8-PM
SCHOOL
CONCERT
TEA

It took a while for my normal buoyancy to return and find a way to cope with my new world. One or two teachers, Lump Lewis especially, had noticeably gone out of their way to put a metaphorical arm around my shoulders.

I quickly discovered the fact that I came from a very poor background was an embarrassingly open secret; free meals, no contribution needed to the school fund, and a uniform allowance, immediately set me apart from most of the others. I carried this stigma unnecessarily heavily for a time.

Chopping off my right thumb in a farmyard accident a year previously at the age of ten probably also helped to get a modest sympathy vote from one or two of the staff. I was also self-conscious about this missing digit for a while, but as I found my feet and developed my own circle of new friends it became an asset rather than a liability: it set me apart. I was inching back to the centre stage, albeit not for the greatest of reasons. Being pretty reasonable at any sport I tried also helped. By the time I left secondary school it was such a part of me that only when people asked how I lost it, did I remember it was missing. The same remains true to this day.

Many years later I stopped at a petrol station with my whole family in the car. I noticed that the attendant filling my tank had one of his thumbs missing. As we drove away, I said

"That poor chap back there has only got one thumb."

Only when my children erupted with laughter from the back of the car, did I realise the irony of what I had said.

In 1952, when I was ten years old, I sat for something called the Eleven Plus exam, along with all the other kids at Rushall Church of England Primary School. This exam was eventually largely abolished by a Labour Government appalled that those who passed were subsequently treated differently to those who failed. There can be no winners and no losers in this life. Perish the thought. Only much later did I understand that politicians the world over promote policies that encourage their re-election. Grammar school pupils typically voted Tory.

Bill Gates gave a talk at a high school recently where he is quoted as saying: "Your school may have done away with winners and losers, but life has not."

Where I grew up, he would have been greeted warmly as the first Yank that anyone locally had seen in the flesh, but received less acclamation for voicing an opinion that was so self-evident. No-one in my village believed for a moment that all people had been created equal.

Rushall was then, as now, a tiny sleepy village in rural Wiltshire nestling snugly at the north eastern foot of the Salisbury Plain with a contented population of some one hundred and fifty souls. Halfway between the ancient stone piles of Stonehenge and Avebury, everyone seemed to have lived there since time began. Tithe records show the village having a similar population of around one hundred and fifty during the 1300s. Perhaps there were natural balancing forces at work?

Most adult men, including my stepfather, were farm labourers who came from a long line of farm labourers who had toiled over the same ground for centuries. Tractors were just replacing horses, but there remained much manual work. Most adult women worked from morning until night cooking, cleaning, mending, washing, scrubbing, knitting, darning for their husbands and children, just as their mothers and grandmothers had done before them.

The primary school drew children from other villages and had over one hundred pupils shared between 2 ½ teachers. The ½ was the headmaster, whose main role appeared to us to be the regular caning of male miscreants, and the paying of special attention to the female pupils as they undertook their afternoon sporting activities.

"Higher with those legs, girls," became a standing copycat chant among us lads.

In living memory only three children had passed the Eleven Plus from Rushall Church of England School. The headmaster's son, who most thought had received some special assistance, a daughter from one of the three rich families in the village, and Master Pitcher. (One of my village chums insists that I was the first person to pass 'properly', but my recollections are different.) Interestingly, it came out in a study conducted in 1957 that children from middle class families were more likely to get grammar school places than those from families lower down the social order. Some questions were apparently slanted towards that end asking, for example, for knowledge regarding the role of household servants or classical composers. I don't recall I had any questions on either, thank goodness.

Although I had no way of knowing it at the time, it was a major life-changing moment. Two of my best friends at the time, who subsequently became lifetime buddies, failed and went to Pewsey Secondary School, subsequently leading very different lives. Not necessarily better or worse, but certainly very different.

"I've got something a little out of the ordinary for you this time," Lump Lewis said encouragingly. We are back to 1959 and the DGS careers room.

In those days there were two inviolate laws about employment after school. First, you had to get a job; being unemployed was absolutely not an option. Going on the dole (that's Job Seekers Allowance to you youngsters) was unthinkable and guaranteed to bring shame, scandal and derision on the whole family. Especially for parents whose son had been to the Grammar. "All that reading and learning wasted," would have been among the kinder admonishments.

Secondly, jobs outside of insurance, banking, the armed forces, teaching or the civil service just didn't appear on any radar screens. I'd previously considered all of them:

¤ Insurance – the actuarial exams sounded worse than following in my stepfather's footsteps.

¤ Banking – quill pens and no sunlight? I was used to fresh air.

¤ Armed forces – liked the sound of all the sporting opportunities but I might get killed.

¤ Civil service – difficult to understand what this involved, but the brochures had boredom written all over them.

¤ Teaching – did not have the patience for it, and anyway I wanted to leave school.

And I really did want to leave school. All my old mates from the village had left at the normal age of fifteen and were now earning money. In the sixth form, school trips were common and popular. I could not go on any of them because they required cash; this simple resource that my parents and I lacked.

I didn't mind too much most of the time, to tell the truth. While I had, over the years, built a new circle of friends at the grammar school, I was still happiest with my old village chums and I never tired of the simple and free pleasures that Rushall and its surroundings had to offer.

However, there was one exception. This concerned a proposed field trip to Paris, with the official prime purpose of improving the participants' language skills. But all the talk behind the bike shed was of obtaining a copy of D.H. Lawrence's scandalous novel *Lady Chatterley's Lover*. This was still banned in the UK but readily available in the unexpurgated version from the much more liberal bookshops of

France. Oh, to get one's hands on one of these. Could it be as exciting as all the reports suggested? An American senator had written of it: "It is most damnable! It is written by a man with a diseased mind and a soul so black that he would obscure even the darkness of hell." What more could a naive sixteen-year-old yearn for?

So I had to wait until 1960, after a famous trial allowed full publication in the UK. Although I had been an avid reader of D.H. Lawrence for several years previously, somehow this particular fruit from his pen did not taste quite so juicy once it was no longer forbidden.

Hard cash: that one ingredient that was preventing me from having a perfect adolescence. Not much, but enough for the basic essentials: booze, fags, wheels, and girls. My best chat up line at the time involved asking the young lady in question whether she might care to meet me at the edge of the cornfield after school. Not the best snog-catcher, I can assure you. If only I could have learnt from Mellors' experiences earlier in my life!

No-one, not parents, friends, or teachers ever mentioned the possibility of university to me, even though I completed my schooldays with more than sufficient O and A levels. And I never raised it with myself. I wanted to get out there, have some readies in my pocket and start "raking for that gurt cheese." Fame and fortune beckoned. It was waiting for me out there somewhere. Looking back, it was probably for the best. My feet were too itchy for the unknown world outside to keep patience with yet more learnin'.

Lump Lewis again: "Are you with me Pitcher? Have a look at this."

"This" was a brochure from Barclays Dominian, Colonial and Overseas Limited. Honestly, that's what the overseas arm of Barclays Bank was called in those days. The booklet was well designed for moonraker dreamers like me. It was crammed with photographs of exotic locations. Blindingly white bank branches were framed by sun-kissed beaches, backed by rich green palm trees swaying gently in hot, tropical breezes. I'd seen similar locations in the movies, but this was for real… and it looked glorious.

The pay was good. They demanded at least two A levels. I was hooked.

"Where do I sign, sir?" I spluttered. This was it. Just let me get started raking for that big, shiny, yeller, tropical moon!

"Thought we might have found it at long last," Lump nodded sagely and with a somewhat relieved tone.

Chapter 2: Learning the game

And so it was that I duly presented myself outside the forbidding closed front doors of Barclays Bank, Pewsey Branch at 8.58am on a bright autumnal morning in September 1960. I had never been inside a bank in my life before, but at the ripe old age of seventeen, I had got the job.

OK, so there were no swaying palm trees or sun kissed, golden sands. The small print in the brochure said that you couldn't be sent abroad with Barclays Dominian, Colonial and Overseas Limited until you were twenty-one. But I'd seen a glimpse of that gurt tropical moon and I could dream of heaven for a few more years.

This was my first proper job. I had worked as a paperboy since the age of eleven for twelve shillings and sixpence a week before travelling eight miles by winding service bus to school in Devizes from Monday to Friday. It was through this role that I acquired one great skill that I retain to this day. Some of the dogs on my round were ferocious. Think of the *Hound of the Baskervilles* and treble it. I tried to swap routes with one of my best friends who, with great good fortune, had drawn all pussy cats, teddy bears and the best-looking village girls. I tried pleading with the newsagent using hereditary cowardice as an excuse, but he would brook no debate. This was not America with its natty boxes outside the front gate. This was "put them all the way through the letter boxes on the front door, or I'll find someone who will." The local builder's mansion was the worst.

- three slobbering beasts -

It was guarded by three slobbering beasts never matched before or since in any horror film you may care to name. They had free rein over the large garden. The driveway from the impressive wrought-iron front gates to the solid oak main door was at least one hundred yards. I was terrified every morning as I unlatched the front gate, closed my eyes, walked shaking towards the front door, felt for the letterbox, deposited my cargo, and forced myself to walk equally steadily all the way back. The dogs never left me, growling, slavering and tugging at my school uniform every step of the way. But, over time, it got better. They came to realise both that I was incapable of doing them harm and that, abjectly scared though I felt inside, I was not going to give them any good sport by running in circles like a startled rabbit. Nowadays, it's like a Crocodile Dundee movie. Dogs have only to look into my eyes and they collapse like docile water buffalo at my feet.

In the summers I worked on the farm as temporary harvest labour, starting at seven in the morning and usually finishing just as the sun was setting. Often a fourteen hour day for three pounds and ten shillings a week. I loved it. Open air and good, honest manual toil. My best lesson with this job came from the weary, worldly wise, battle-hardened, permanent farm workers.

"You work too hard," they chided. "Go more slowly. Them bales will still be there tomorrow and ye be showing the rest of us up."

I'm not sure I ever heeded their warnings, but it did expose my naivety and showed me at an early stage that most people play political games much better than I was ever able to master throughout the whole of my life. I left banking briefly in the early 1960s to join the so-called management development programme of a well known civil engineering company based in London. They were going through a fallow period. There was virtually no work and little need to develop new management as a consequence. So many staff had been shed that when prospective customers came in to see the firm's operations at first hand, bodies were moved from floor to floor just ahead of their progress to give the impression we were bursting at the seams with business. I thought this was such a nonsense that I left and re-joined banking. The best career move I was ever to make. Thank goodness I didn't become a politician!

So, back to the front door of Barclays, Pewsey Branch. I remember three things before the day even got started.

First, my clothes. I had never owned a suit. Banks demanded such attire. Neither my parents nor I could afford a new one. So my mother had bought me a second-hand one for £4 from the local headmaster's son (yes, the very same as passed the Eleven Plus). He was a good four inches taller than me, broader all round, and smoked like a trooper. My white shirt had suffered several years of school service and my only pair of shoes had kicked endless cans around the playground. I looked like something out of *Les Miserables* and smelt like yesterday's bonfire.

Secondly, I arrived after cycling four miles on my second hand bike. Thankfully it was not raining that day. Only the gentry had cars in our village. There was nowhere to put it, so I plonked it against the front wall. My first potential black mark from the manager, as I was soon to learn.

Thirdly, my mother had insisted on preparing me a packed lunch as all village women had done for their menfolk since time began.

Bread, cheese and a flask of cold, black, sugarless tea bounced around in my faded school satchel. I was tense enough already, but I became even more agitated as I wondered where I was going to eat this little picnic. And anyway, was the fare likely to enhance my image? I thought not.

I rang the bell. John B, the head clerk I later discovered, opened the door.

"Come on in. That your bike? Park it down the side alleyway otherwise he'll go berserk when he gets back."

"Good news," he continued "Old Man's playing golf with customers today so we can go when we balance. We're pretty busy, so just hang around the office and pick up what you can. Should have more time to spend with you tomorrow, all being well."

After that I did nothing all day apart from sit and watch and listen. It was a five-man branch including the manager and yours truly. John C was the one cashier, and Heather R's job was called machinist. We were light years away from the world of grand titles for ordinary jobs. Heather was a bonus; we had been to grammar school together – and she was female. She had been in the 'A' stream, but I didn't hold this against her, having realised at an early stage that at the Devizes Grammar School all working class pupils were automatically placed in the 'B' stream. It was the straw sticking out of our ears, you know!

Lunchtime came and went. We all sat in the manager's office apart from John C, who remained on counter duty until we could rotate. I was relieved that the others also had packed lunches albeit with more exotic contents than mine.

"Old Man hates it, but this is where we are entitled to eat every day," intoned John B. "Bank rules are that there has to be a place inside, away from customers, where we can have our lunch. And there's nowhere else in this bloody little bunker."

John B had done National Service and was therefore qualified to talk like this. Conscription made men of boys, or so it seemed when you were barely more than a child yourself.

The branch was tiny. In those days the offices of banks, solicitors and accountants were deliberately kept shabby and unassuming lest customers should think their fees were being swallowed up in unnecessary extravagance and frivolous ostentation. How times have changed.

No, our branch wasn't just small - it was minute. Customer space was a narrow corridor leading straight from the front door, the short counter was iron-barred to the ceiling to prevent villains jumping over I later learned, and the back office was the size of a largish bathroom. The manager's office, the strong room and a little storage room out back, and that was it.

All branches opened at ten o'clock in the morning and closed at three o'clock in the afternoon with no Saturdays.

"Keep your wits about you. We can all leave once we've balanced," said John B. This meant nothing to me, but at 3.30pm there was a little cheer from the others. Everything was rapidly put away, the strong room locked, and I was on my bike cycling home.

My mother, needless to say, was surprised to see me wheeling my bicycle up the front path. Worried I might only have survived half a day she said, "Everything all right?" I know all mothers worry, especially about only sons, but perhaps mine had more cause than most having fainted when her ten-year-old appeared at the kitchen one day minus a thumb and pouring blood.

"Fine," I replied. "What's for dinner?"

Dinner (confusingly we used the same word to describe the midday meal) was the main eating occasion of the day for country folk. My stepfather worked on a large farm of over 4,000 acres so was rarely home for lunch.

My mother prepared almost everything from scratch. We had no fridge and freezers hadn't yet reached post-war Britain, so everything was freshly prepared. Most villagers kept chickens and a pig at the bottom of the garden; fresh rabbit simply involved a fifty yard chase across the nearest field; beef, lamb, cheese, milk and butter came from the farm; and spare hare, pheasant, partridge, rook and pigeon all went to the farm labourer 'beaters' after the frequent local shoots. Yes, we really did eat all the above. Flour was milled locally. Apples, pears, gooseberries, rhubarb, plums and all vegetables came from the back plot of our tied cottage. Fish came from the river and a local delivery van that called once a week. Starve we did not!

Catching a rabbit, by the way, was easier than might be imagined. Although when first startled they would burst away using four pawed sidesteps better than anything you've seen from an international rugby fly half, they tired rapidly. So long as we could keep them away from dense hedges and coverts, our young legs would soon outlast theirs. I caught many that didn't make the bunnies try-line but I never killed one; that was my stepfather's job. I carried them back home, holding their two rear legs tightly together while they wriggled upside down like a bob tailed Houdini in a straitjacket. He would quickly stretch them out over his knee. One hand pulled the hind legs, the other stretched the head over the fulcrum his leg had created, and the neck was broken faster than … well, let's just say very quickly. My mother would hang them upside down straightaway, break their rear legs and pull the fur off downwards in one firm, continuous motion. If their bodies were still warm it all came away in one piece without any effort. Into the pot with carrots, onions and gravy, and another culinary delight was on its way. Hares were a different quarry altogether. They could outrun us until eternity, and they knew it. I tried a few times, but never succeeded. I swear they used to look back and grin sometimes as they slowed just enough to give the chaser hope, before re-engaging top gear and 'haring' into the distance.

'Tied' meant that the house went with the job and could be repossessed the instant any worker left the farm. In practice, I can only recall one instance of a labourer moving on to better himself. Most stayed put for the whole of their lives. There was hardly any mobility. Generations had lived and died in the same small cluster of villages, marriage often being the only reason for moving a mile or so from one to the next. None of the workers had cars and the rural bus service was expensive, so most people travelled to the nearest town of any size – Devizes – very infrequently. Some of the old timers had hardly strayed outside the village for the whole of their lives. Amazingly, looking back, this did not prevent them from having views about anything and everything happening on the planet.

Vegetables came from the back garden and were gathered and eaten in season. Lettuce in the spring, peas in summer, brussel sprouts picked with the frost hard on them in the winter and so on. If we didn't grow it, then we didn't know it existed. I was in my mid-teens before I saw my first bananas and pineapples at Devizes market. Enough potatoes were grown to last the whole year. They were cooked straight from the ground until early autumn, then all dug up and stored in total darkness in the cupboard under the stairs. One of my earliest jobs at home involved crawling into this black space from time to time during the winter months and removing any budding shoots from the pile of spuds. Left untended, they started growing of their own accord and their insides turned into a black, putrid liquid. The musky smell has never left me.

Another of my home tasks was latrine duty with my stepfather. We had one toilet. It was a bucket under a wooden seat in a shed at the bottom of the garden. No flush, needless to say, and our sole water supply was one cold tap in the scullery. So the treasures of the bucket had to be buried in the back garden once a week. Sometimes, in very hot weather, a combination of the flies and the fermenting contents demanded more frequent attention.

It seemed to do no harm to the vegetables: I used to eat peas and broad beans raw from their pods and carrots straight from the ground. Delicious!

The village school also had no flushing toilets. Just two rows of wooden cubicles – one for the boys and one for the girls – with each little compartment having a hole in a wooden seat and a metal bucket beneath. My stepfather volunteered to empty these once a week and once again I was commandeered into service as the bog cleaner's assistant. It was dirty work, but someone had to do it!

This was even less pleasant than the cottage latrine duty. First, kids being kids, many of the users would have failed the Bomber Command recruitment test. Secondly, the buckets were extracted by means of a continuous horizontal channel, exiting through a small side door. This was where yours truly came in most useful. Think of a boy chimney sweep going up and down collecting soot; but this time the task involved crawling on the flat concrete floor. The buckets were full to overflowing, the floor was uneven creating spillages to shame a major oil company, the smell was far removed from the scent of jasmine floating across the sacred river, and it was not black soot covering my clothes when the job was done.

The only thing that made it slightly bearable was that we buried the stuff in the headmaster's garden. Somehow, there seemed to be a little more slopping over the tops of the buckets as we carried them across his front lawn ... and we refrained from digging the hole quite so deep. Didn't seem to harm his vegetables either though.

When I got married a few years later at the age of twenty-two (having asked for and obtained the Bank's mandatory permission first) I bought my first house near Bracknell in Berkshire, which was a new town developed largely for overspill Londoners. It cost £5,200: this seemed an unbelievably vast sum, but a subsidised bank mortgage helped to stop me from choking too much. The semi was a new build with the front and back gardens left for the owners to establish and cultivate. My plot was devoted totally to vegetables because I thought that was what rear gardens were intended for. In no time my new neighbours were knocking on my door asking to examine what was going on at the rear of my property. They had never seen onions, cabbages, runner beans, carrots, and so on actually growing before. I should have charged an entrance fee. And we had flushing toilets!

So, my first day of rakin' didn't change very much. I was still a country bumpkin enjoying the warm security of our small cottage and the simple joys of the verdant countryside of the Pewsey Vale. The most fertile valley in Europe, local people used to say. We kids accepted this statement as our gospel since we had never been to anywhere else in Europe. Most had only a vague notion of where the Continent was on the map. Was there anything worth seeing outside of our lovely county anyway?

And I still had all of my local friends, two of whom are blood brothers to this day. I think I would need the literary skills of a laureate to explain it fully, but growing up in that close-knit, all-enveloping, self-sufficient community created images and bonds that have remained strong and clear throughout the whole of my life. One of my great joys is returning to this land of my roots as I do from time to time, and re-discovering on every trip that I'm treated just the same as ever by people who knew me when I was young. How could it be otherwise, since they have thankfully seen nothing of me outside that childhood pattern? I have tales to tell, but so do they. Tickling a trout from the local river and selling it back to the farmer beats the spots off travels to far distant lands with strange sounding names.

Chapter 3: It's so easy

Meanwhile, back at the branch....

I spent the entire first week filing away papers. At that time all cheques and other vouchers specific to an individual account were sent back to customers with their statements. So, the large pile of paper slips emanating from each day's work had to be accurately filed. If this task was not done properly first time around it caused no end of trouble when statements came to be mailed, because all the appropriate vouchers had to be found before despatch. If they were not in the right slot, then there were only another 1,999 accounts to look through: a powerful incentive not to be slipshod.

Sounds boring, tedious, repetitive, soul-destroying? Yes! Sounds easy? No!

Back then, cheques and credit slips carried no personalised information. Although they looked grand affairs with the bank's name in ornate, copper-plate script along the top, and a large blue oval government duty stamp in the top right quadrant, they contained no printed details regarding a customer's name or account number (the latter had not yet been invented, causing older customers in later years to beg to be referred to by name and not by number). The tax per cheque, by the way, was tuppence as it had been since 1918. Somewhat surprisingly, given governments' propensity to attach a levy to anything that moves and most of what does not, it was abolished in 1971.

Those funny little blobby figures you see in a line at the bottom of today's cheques – known in the trade as magnetic ink character recognition, or MICR for short – did not cross the pond to Britain until later in the 1960s more's the pity.

So, each item had to be identified from a customer's signature and any other clues the little grey cells could fathom. Perhaps a distinctive type of ink or an unmistakeable hand?

We had around 2,000 customers. Any day's entries could run to around 1,000 pieces of paper. The filing drawers were heavy, wooden, old-fashioned affairs with dog-eared, cardboard dividers used to separate individual names. Space was at a premium in the office, and these drawers were already full to overflowing, leaving little room for more paper or chubby fingers.

It was the worst job in the branch. But it was how everyone had started since time immemorial. I was the junior, this was part of my lot, and it remained so until I moved on from Pewsey ten months later. Worse than the boredom was when I made a mistake.

"There's a cheque missing from my statement" was only slightly less heart stopping than "You sent me Bill Jones' credit slips with my statement."

"Putting you on the waste next week, Mike," John B informed me on the Friday as we were leaving for the weekend, "then you can start to call yourself a bank clerk."

This was the occupation I put in my first passport and every other official document for years after. Now even the cleaner is a 'banker'. I was still hesitating to use this moniker to describe myself when I eventually retired as vice chairman, Asia Pacific, in 1999.

I had no idea what the waste was, but it could only imply some modest advancement on my filing duties. Surely it couldn't in any way refer to some even more ghastly activity involving the branch garbage bags, or even worse, be an extension of my village latrine duties?

I was already beginning to realise that formal training in a modern sense was non-existent. You were vaguely pointed towards a task and pretty much left to work it out for yourself. Clearly this approach had some basis in the way your more senior workmates had themselves learnt the ropes, but I think there was also an element to do with drawing the veils of knowledge and understanding back slowly. Information was power. Climbing the rungs of the promotion ladder which existed back then was a slow and carefully delineated process. Make things happen too quickly and you might fall off, or worse, be stepped on by someone else attempting to clamber past.

It may sound strange to today's ear, but this very crude style of yesteryear did encourage and develop the use of personal initiative. You worked things out for yourself, made your own mistakes and realised that successfully rakin' for the moon was going to be largely down to No.1. I count it as a further piece of great good fortune that there has never been a time in my life when I have ever been led to believe that the world owed me a living, or that anyone else was to blame for my decisions or actions. As William Ernest Henley so eloquently put it:

> "It matters not how strait the gate,
> How charged with punishments the scroll,
> I am the master of my fate,
> I am the captain of my soul."

The waste (I have no idea of the derivation of this word) proved to be a large pad of closely columned sheets with around thirty headings per page, most of which meant little if anything to me. In truth, the only item I recognised was headed 'cash', none of which as yet had I been allowed to see, let alone touch.

"Just remember every credit must have a debit, and every debit must have a credit," instructed John B as if this were all the tuition anyone but a complete dunderhead could need. Then with the merest of grins "oh, and the credits are nearest to the window." Finally the faintly menacing "Remember, none of us can go home until you've got the wretched thing to agree."

I said nothing in reply, but knew I was going to torture this thing into agreement when the doors closed, if that's what it took for us all to get out early.

The cramped back office was Dickensian. I sat on a tall stool with the waste pad in front of me on a sloping wooden desk. Ballpoints were not allowed in the bank back then. Approved nibbed pens were dipped in ink pots filled with a mixture we concocted ourselves from powder supplied by our mysterious central stationery department. Once by mistake, I ordered 5,000 deposit slips printed in Welsh from this faceless unit. The manager was not amused because the branch was charged for every item. At least I made a very small contribution to keeping the language alive.

I had to ask Heather quite a few times on the first day which columns to post the various items in, but I quickly got the hang of it. Later, after I started my bookkeeping module as part of the compulsory banking exams, I understood that this was a daybook or day journal. Every transaction of whatever description undertaken by the branch that day was recorded in the waste in some form or another. At the end of each day it had to 'agree' or balance since every item had to have a credit and an equal and opposite debit. I felt a little like the mission control or Captain Kirk. "Beam me up, Scottie, whisk me to that tropical paradise I saw in the brochure," I silently pleaded.

"Don't forget to sub-total in pencil as you go along," John B again. "It'll make it much easier at close of business, and we want to keep getting out by 3.30 while the Old Man's not here."

So, no pressure then, I thought.

There were two features of life in those days which I need to startle younger readers with at this point. First, we used pounds, shillings and pence; twenty shillings to the pound, and twelve pence to the shilling. Decimalisation of the currency was not introduced until 1971. In case it's been keeping you puzzled from a page or so back, it was this change which prompted the abolition of the duty on each cheque. The Government had promised that prices would not increase as a result of decimalisation, and 'tuppence' simply could not be manipulated in any sensible fashion to meet this guarantee.

Secondly, we had no computers. Not just Pewsey branch, but the whole bank functioned without an electronic chip in sight. Virtually everything was a manual operation.

We did have one very slow and noisy mechanical adding machine – an Adler I think it was – operated by punching buttons and pulling down a side lever much like a fruit machine. But it was cumbersome to work with and banned from use by the manager on the basis that adding up long columns of figures in one's head was good for the soul of every aspiring bank clerk during their formative years. It was rumoured that some old-timers could add up all three columns of pounds, shillings and pence simultaneously faster than you can punch numbers into your smart-phone.

By the end of the first week I had learnt the basics of double entry bookkeeping without even knowing what it was called. Far less that it was invented in Florence as early as the thirteenth century. And I can still add up lines of figures in my head faster than most shop assistants work their calculators. Not bad considering that at the start of the job I had never seen a cheque book or a bank statement before in my life.

"off for the cash as usual, boys?"

POST
OFFICE

I was now deemed responsible enough for one other job. Once a fortnight two male members of staff, one always had to be the head clerk, were despatched to collect a supply of new banknotes from the local post office. There was no little ceremony attached to this task. We were initialled in and out of the bank building by the manager ("I counted them in, and I counted them back"), a heavy metal chain was attached to a portable strong-box and then secured around our waists, and lastly we were each handcuffed to the chain.

"Remember, Head Office Instructions say you must vary your route each time," intoned the manager, "and no heroics if you're attacked."

I must have worn a slightly startled expression as I looked at John B. I was only somewhat reassured when I saw him give a little wink at me outside the manager's line of sight.

We had only gone a few yards down the High Street when John stopped, took a key from his pockets and undid the cuffs and proceeded to light up a cigarette, handing me one as he did so.

"Silly sod," he said. "He always goes through that routine for show. He knows there's only one way to get to the post office, and I'm not going to have my arm chopped off by some cheap crook for Barclays or anyone."

One of our regular customers was passing by and accepted a cigarette from John's offered packet. "Off for the cash as usual, boys?" he enquired.

I looked at John. The three of us laughed. "South America here we come," chuckled John.

So, to the weekend. It wasn't going to be Latin America. What did I do for fun? Well, while at Pewsey branch my social life hardly changed, save in one respect. I had a little cash.

I was still living with my parents as an only child. As was expected of working class children, I was now paying them thirty shillings for board and lodging from my weekly pay of around seven pounds. But that still left more money in my pocket than I had ever seen before.

The first splurge was on a car. I had learnt the basics while driving tractors on the farm during my early teenage years and a distant step cousin had got me through the formal test by taking me out in his dilapidated Hillman on Sunday mornings. He poached pheasants with his unlicensed shotgun through the open passenger window as we drifted along those wonderfully hedged and heavily scented Wiltshire lanes. He would spot his target, motion for me to slow down, fire, mark his kill and call for me to speed up and continue driving. After a while, when he was happy no-one had spotted us, I would undertake a three-point turn (OK, maybe it took a few more, but who's counting?). I would then retrace our route, he would jump out to collect the spoils of his illegal work and off we sped. Butch Cassidy and the Sundance Kid, moonraker style. And all with learner plates!

Interestingly, most of the farm workers never had to pass any sort of driving test because their jobs were deemed to be in the national interest. This worked fine on a hundred-acre field, but sometimes less well on public roads. My stepfather was once fined for driving a tractor without due care and attention when he turned left into a lane, towing an enormous load of bales of hay. His trailer was equipped with neither lights nor indicators and of course he had no rear view whatsoever. A low-slung sports car with an open top, being driven too fast by some natty gent in blazer and flannels accompanied by the obligatory lady passenger with long, flowing blonde hair, skidded almost right underneath his wagon. No one was hurt, but Johnny sports car had a better lawyer.

"Baint right." My stepfather had never been so upset. "Baint right." I don't think he ever fully recovered from what to him was yet another example of "it's the rich wot gets the pleasure".

Another dimension to their 'national interest' role was that many were excused active military service during the war. Instead they were required to join the Home Guard, or Dad's Army. They were allowed to keep their uniforms, gas masks and other bits and pieces when the war ended. These became props for the lads of the village and for a number of years afterwards unsuspecting adults could be walking their dogs in the woods suddenly to be surrounded by a battalion of daubed young faces tripping over army uniforms that had clearly been made for much larger human beings.

My first car was a rusting hulk of an Austin 8. I paid the princely sum of £10. Then, as now, I knew nothing about the mysteries of motors, but one of my village chums with a mechanical bent was by then working for a firm of agricultural engineers in Devizes. Somehow he got the beast in running order and improved the exterior enormously with carefully applied coatings of Fordson blue and Ferguson grey paint. Don't ask!

I did hundreds of miles in that car all over the country with enough tales to fill another book. Most will have to await that day, but as a taster, I did once lose a rear wheel on the Chiswick Flyover in heavy traffic one busy Monday morning. From my rear view mirror I saw the wheel gradually receding as it bounced from one car to another. Bruce Willis, eat your heart out!

For some reason I cannot now recall clearly, I avoided telling my parents that I was the proud owner of a car. I kept it at a friend's house in the adjoining village. I think it was probably because at first sight it was such an ugly heap that it didn't really fit the image my mother was building up in the village of "how well Michael is doing at the bank". Words and figures differ, to coin a phrase familiar to bank workers the world over. Of course, in that environment nothing stayed secret for very long and all was soon exposed. But at least by then my car's colours matched the passing tractors!

The second necessary spend was on a new suit. It was already painfully apparent that the headmaster's son and I had very different builds, and anyway, I was just beginning to see the first glimmerings of the good life. To my green eyes, the other members of staff and most of our customers were dressed like something out of a fashion magazine. I wanted some too.

There was only one place to go for haute couture in those days: The Brittox, Devizes, the Oxford Street of our existence. My first new suit ... and made to measure, no less. I learnt some time later from a school chum, who worked there on Saturdays, that local tailors loved the particular chain store I was gracing with my custom. In spite of supposedly careful measurement in the shop, when things came back from their main factory in the north of England, very little fitted and the retailer had to pay local experts to put things right.

Like most other customers, I bought the suit on credit. The suit cost £7 and I paid it off at £1 a month. This was the norm, so there was no shame or embarrassment in the transaction.

I made one serious mistake. The Beatles were just starting to become famous and I bought an all-together-too-snazzy Paul

McCartney look-alike with fake Italian styling and a mock silk sky-blue lining. As soon as I wore it to work, I knew the error of my ways. It just wasn't right for a bank clerk. John B had a quick word, and it was back to The Brittox for a second bout of tick that I could ill afford.

I eventually sold the car for £11 (the only time I've made a profit on a motor). I can't remember what happened to the first new suit: I probably buried it in a dung heap one dark moonlit night. Dreams do not always progress in a straight line.

The third necessary expenditure was on my banking exams, organised by The Institute of Bankers, Lombard Street, London. These were obligatory, especially if you worked for D, C & O as it was colloquially known, because they would not send you abroad until you had made solid progress with them. Yes, the thought of those dusky maidens singing softly under swaying palm trees was not forgotten as I filed vouchers and 'agreed' the waste.

This work had to be done in your own time and at your own expense, although there were modest grants once you passed. Since I lived many miles away from the nearest technical college offering relevant courses, I did it all through the post using specialised correspondence training firms. They sent you reading material, and you returned homework on a regular basis, which came back through the mail marked and tutored. There was no other contact whatsoever, which was just as well since we had no telephone at home and using the local call box on a damp November evening would not have been terribly conducive to study.

Most people found this a tough way of learning. But I had been an avid reader for as long as I could remember, and I liked working without someone pouring over me the whole time. One of my several weaknesses is that I've never taken to being closely coached, much preferring to work things through for myself. I was also good at exams. This is not necessarily the same as being bright. At school, I would spend more time than most thinking about the end purpose of all the blather in the classroom, which was of course to get through the various tests and examinations.

Another beneficial element to this type of study was that it was very quiet at home. I was a sort of only child. I have never met my real father and know next to nothing about him. I looked upon my stepfather as the paternal figure, although in truth parents in Rushall in those days had not yet received the Hollywood makeover treatment. They were there to feed you, dig you out of any deep trouble and not enquire too closely into what you might be up to when you were not indoors.

My mother was of Scottish stock. My maternal grandparents were born in the bleak Orkneys but moved to the slums of Edinburgh for work. To be entirely accurate, they moved to sunny Leith, so called my mother said because the sun never shone there. I met them both a couple of times: my grandmother seemed quiet to the point of meekness, perhaps because my grandfather was a loud, burly, larger-than-life man.

"Ack, he was a right tartar to us kids," my mother used to say, without going into any further detail. Throughout the whole of her life she was extremely tight-lipped about her history and therefore my very early years.

I was in the village hall for a social night when I was fifteen and I overheard a couple of local biddies talking about me. They didn't know I was listening. "He's got two sisters around, you know," said one.

"Oh, I mind them well. Pretty things," replied the other. "Where are they now?"

"Be with their dad still," explained the first knowingly. "They be a few miles away down Manningford way."

This was the first I had ever heard about having siblings. My mother had never told me anything about them and I never mentioned the conversation to her until many decades later. It's difficult to explain why. I think it was mainly that I didn't want to upset her by raising a past she clearly didn't want to discuss. Perhaps I was also enjoying being an 'only'?

I have met each of my sisters once on separate occasions. One came visiting from America looking for her mother and I supplied the conduit telephone number. The other came to her funeral. People sometimes say they find this lack of contact strange, but you don't miss that which you have never had. And looking back, it did help those banking studies.

So I ended up with a few distinctions and the accolade of finishing in the top ten for my year (actually I was tenth). Several years later, this placing entitled me to try for something called the Transatlantic Banking Scholarship. I was the first Barclays winner and spent a year in the USA studying their banking systems. I was twenty-four, and the journey from Heathrow to JFK was my first-ever flight in an aeroplane.

Perhaps if I had been out playing with my sisters most evenings, I would never have started my lifelong love affair with the American part of my moondreams?

Chapter 4: Everyday

But I get ahead of myself. Back to basics.

While I could not pretend for one second that I was using any of the theories drummed into me during my two years' study of maths, chemistry and geography at A level, I was becoming a bit of a wizard at agreeing the waste. And the figures showed me a lot about what went on throughout the branch, since just about every activity had to be converted to figures and pass through the daily log of which I was the increasingly smug custodian.

As an aside, I never have used any of the vast amount of stuff I spent hours learning by rote during my sixth-form years, and I sometimes wonder how many others would feel the same?

On a similar tack, hardly anyone with a university degree joined a clearing bank in that era. It would have been considered by all and sundry a waste of a hard-earned qualification had any done so. It was many years into my career before I encountered a graduate on the staff of the bank. At the time he was treated with considerable suspicion and disdain. He had an economics degree from Oxford I recall, and was promptly – and properly in most people's minds including my own – incarcerated in the dungeons of our centralised Economics Department. It took him many years to escape. It has left me with a healthy scepticism for much secondary and tertiary education. I am writing this shortly after a Chinese New Year trip to Boracay in the Philippines where the friendly hotel receptionists told me they needed a college degree as a pre-requisite for applying for the job. A hotel receptionist? A degree? Come on!

My progress so far sped my advancement on to two further tasks. One was agreeing the remittances both inwards and outwards, and the second was posting the ledgers. The latter brought my first working encounter with that most mystical and awe-inspiring of all creatures under the sun: The Bank Manager.

Each morning before any of us arrived, a sealed package was deposited in a special lock box which could be opened from the outside by the security firm making the delivery and from the inside by nominated branch staff. It was sealed, had to be opened by two people and was treated with appropriate reverence. This was the Head Office Bag. Even when spoken, the words seemed to deserve capital letters. The process was repeated in reverse each afternoon as we were leaving.

In the morning, the greatest bulk inside the bag was made up of cheques drawn by our customers but paid in at other banks and branches. Amazingly, the sorting of these cheques had been undertaken centrally by hundreds of women (some years later I saw the process in action and, yes, they were all female) using a purely manual operation involving a simple device called an Ampidex tray. Their hands flashed faster than a croupier at a busy blackjack table. They ran several passes using the numbers that you still see on the top right hand corner of cheques. Appropriately, these digits retain the same name: sorting code numbers.

Each cheque had to be examined individually. I was not allowed to undertake this examination task until a couple of years later in my career. Each cheque could be returned for one of thirteen reasons and, rather appropriately for branches in moonraker country, for ease of learning and remembering, the justifications were encapsulated into a mnemonic: S.W.E.D.E.S. and C.L.A.M.P.S. If you are paying any sort of attention you will notice that there's one of the thirteen missing, and that's 'funds'. This task was solely in the hands of the manager, and I never saw him write those life-threatening words 'Refer to Drawer' in the customary red ink without the sternest of expressions on his face.

"Send it back," he would thunder. "Wait till he gets my letter."

The signature on each cheque had to be initialled by the examining clerk, so there was no hiding place if any of the thirteen had been missed. For those of you desperate to know what the other twelve reasons were, please send me a stamped addressed envelope containing a suitable donation to one of my favourite charities and all will be revealed.

I will provide one for nothing to start you off. M stands not for murder but for mutilated. This one is etched on my memory because of the actions of one of my later branch managers. From time to time he could not decide whether to pay a cheque or bounce it. He solved his own indecision by tearing the offending cheque in half and sending it back to the collecting bank with the words 'mutilated cheque' inscribed thereon. Although completely outside the rules, this bought time for him and the customer without damaging either's reputation.

In the afternoon, cheques paid in that day but drawn on other banks and branches were sorted, totalled and despatched by us via the HO Bag, this time travelling in the reverse direction.

The only exceptions were cheques involving a bank branch within walking distance of ours. This was called the local clearing and found favour with me straight away. To save the convoluted route of the HO Bag we simply put these to one side, totalled them and exchanged them face-to-face with the local bank concerned. In our case, we only had one nearby counterparty – Lloyds, just along the street. So, each morning, a lady clerk from the sign of the black horse and myself from the sign of the spread eagle would meet for a pleasant cup of coffee together in a nearby café and exchange our cheques and payments (and hopefully the odd smile or two as well!). As I say, I liked the local clearing.

Many years later, as I was being whisked in an IBM stretch limo from JFK to their intergalactic headquarters in Armonk, New York, to sign one of the largest deals ever transacted at that time for the latest in cheque image recognition technology (it could even electronically read hand written figures in the amount box of cheques) I couldn't help thinking that life used to be so much simpler. But I have to admit the stretch limo beat my Austin 8.

Next, I was elevated to posting the ledgers and my first terrifying encounters with the branch manager: Jerry Philpott.

"Don't paint," he barked as he tore a paper coin-bag marker out of the top of the heavily bound ledger. "Never get anywhere if you paint!"

All customers had every detail of their transactions recorded by hand in a large, weighty ledger where pages could be added and removed only under dual lock and key. They were kept in the strong room overnight. They were so heavy only male staff were allowed to lift them. My task was to record every item, credit or debit, received that day and update each customer's balance, by manual calculation of course. I had to identify the account using only the customer's signature, record all details including the payee's name (a feature often causing much speculation around the office as you may imagine) and 'strike' a new balance. All this was double checked each day against a parallel process undertaken by Heather on a typewriter style gadget that produced something vaguely resembling modern style statements.

Since my ledgers were the ultimate bible, it was vital that no mistakes were made. If there were errors, as there inevitably were from time to time, they had to be corrected neatly using a small cross against the offending calculation and not obliterated using broad strokes from the thickest pen in the tray. In today's parlance, obliteration removed any audit trail.

"Don't paint," meant, "don't try and cover your traces."

Once every six months, at the end of June and December, the ledgers were 'taken out'. Unfortunately this did not mean that they were dumped outside the front door; would that had been so. Instead, it involved totalling all the balances for every customer and agreeing the sum produced with a figure from a slightly mysterious account that recorded in aggregate every transaction, debit and credit, for the period in the branch.

We had to work until any overall difference was less than £1. Normally we left after midnight on those two days. We also had to calculate manually the credit and debit interest due on each account. I won't describe this process to you for fear of incurring your disbelief, but of all the tasks I undertook in my near forty years with Barclays, this was far and away the most numbskulling and soul-destroying. Think about it for a second or so: many balances change every day, interest rates are often amended quite frequently, and these calculations had to be completed manually every six months for each borrower or saver. And they all had to be correct.

Bonuses were years away from being conceived. But on those two nights, the manager would stay with us, albeit closeted in his office until the work had been satisfactorily concluded. He would then hand each of us with some ceremony a £1 Premium Savings

“Don’t paint”

Bond voucher while muttering a few words of approbation. It wasn't done to overly praise staff; they might get ideas above their station. I also well remember the £1 was added to your next monthly salary to allow tax to be deducted.

Incidentally, since the word comes into this text, and although I was a modest beneficiary during the later stages of my career, I have never been a fan of excessive bonuses. A good salary for an honest day's work, with perhaps an occasional addition for exceptional achievement, should be the norm. Over-the-top bonuses corrupt people and organisations. They often encourage behaviour that runs contrary to shareholders' and customers' best interests. My granny could work it out: if I pay you a very large sum of money based on your sales of things that customers neither understand nor need, what is the likely outcome? And if they both comprehend and want them, selling them shouldn't be that difficult, should it?

To balance those comments, I should also acknowledge that banking was a job for life in those times, as long as you stayed with the same employer and refrained from indulging in something unspeakably awful. So in that sense, staff were motivated by the system to play a long game, carrying no incentive to indulge in silly short-termism. Promotion or demotion was largely on merit, but it has to be admitted that even the significantly incompetent were found a job somewhere within the organisation, as long as there was no hint of dishonesty. The bank was a large and broad church and a hopeless cashier could end up being found a slot running the in-house rowing club for instance, or a bad lender could be transferred to the clearing department, or even better, depending on how one viewed it, the deepest colonies.

But in the meantime, I was enjoying the early finishes. I was getting on well with my colleagues, John B in particular. He had a small motorbike and in good weather we would often go straight from work to swim in the local swimming pool or the nearby river. One summer afternoon after a particularly early finish, I jumped on his pillion and we motored the short few miles to Milk Hill, a mile or so north of Alton Barnes. Here lies one of the famous Wiltshire White Horses. This particular one was completed in 1812, no doubt by male villagers looking for an excuse to get away from their ladies for a weekend.

A short walk from the road and we were on the gigantic horse cut out of the white chalk hill. We both sat down on the large, grassy eye. It was clear and hot; one of those rare days when the air shimmers and the Earth feels as if it has ceased rotating. The northern edge of Salisbury Plain beckoned from several miles away.

My next visit to the same spot came fifty years later. It was another beautiful day and there, spread beneath the horse on the floor of the valley, was an enormous and intricate crop circle. Its canvas was the whole of one large field. It was unbelievable. Perfectly symmetrical and wonderfully detailed.

"What's that?" enquired my girlfriend.

"It's called a crop circle," I said, "it's another thing that Wiltshire is famous for."

"What are those coaches," she went on, "and all the people?"

"Oh, folks come from all over the place to see something like this. It's a bit like birdwatchers – they text each other and drop everything to come and get a sighting."

"Who made it?" she continued, "it's amazing." The heat haze danced before our eyes. The air was thick as cream.

"Took me a long time," I replied. "Let's go and have a drink at The Barge in Honeystreet. Look you can see it just peeping out from behind those trees."

"We might meet some fellow Croppies," I continued. "It's what they call us crop circle geniuses."

She gave me one of those Oscar winning impenetrable looks that the Chinese learn at birth.

"Crazy Gweilo," she muttered. "Let's go, I like honey."

It was the same pub that John B and I had gone to all those years previously. Originally built to quench the thirst of the hard working navvies who build the Kennet and Avon Canal in the early nineteenth century. And have you ever heard of a lovelier name for a village?

I was already getting fed up with my lot at Pewsey branch, and over the second pint I turned to John B: "I joined to see the world," I complained. But he encouraged me to stay, saying that he had never seen anyone pick up the basics so quickly. He's long since passed away, but I owe him a debt.

I kept all my local activities going during this period. My small village amazingly boasted a brass band. I had played the cornet with them since I was eight. I was useless musically, but my two other chums played and it was good to star at fetes, carnivals, remembrance services and the like.

I was always keen on sport and had recently dropped soccer – having decided I was never going to be as good as my idol Ernie Hunt at Swindon Town FC – to play rugby for Devizes on the wing. I was quick in those days and managed to score a few tries when and if the ball eventually came out to me.

My school sweetheart, whom I married a few years later, had gone to Bristol to study at a teacher training college, so my newly acquired wheels enabled me to make that trip in relative comfort from time to time.

Life was not bad therefore, but was I moving fast enough forwards to fame and fortune, let alone swaying palm trees? Perhaps meeting the manager more frequently would speed my progress to the top?

Chapter 5: Look at me

Ask anyone who was involved in retail banking at that time about their first manager. Like first love, they will know the time and place of the first meeting and be able to describe everything about the man in the finest detail. I say 'the man' because there were no lady managers at all at that time in banking. Such a notion was unthinkable. Could a woman become Pope? The glass ceiling was made of concrete. Women were not created to have careers; as soon as the babies came along – which was quite early in most cases in those days before the pill – they would leave and attend to their motherly duties. That was how things were meant to be, or so the perceived wisdom of the time had us believe.

Jerry Philpott was a role model for Captain Mainwaring in *Dad's Army* long before Arthur Lowe captured the part to perfection. Every time I see the TV programme my past life at Pewsey flashes before my eyes.

He was short, stout, pompous, full of his own self-importance, and bustled around the office as if he were chairman of the Board. His military moustache quivered when he barked his commands. His thinning hair was so slicked down that not a hair was ever out of place and his scalp gleamed. He would never be seen in Boots the Chemist to replace bottles of his noxious hair lotion, so that became one of my early errands. Objections would have been unconscionable. I was the office junior and I had to understand my place, just as he would have done some thirty-five years previously. What was the point of all those years of sweat and toil and drudgery, struggling up the ladder, if you couldn't treat today's new entrants as you yourself had been treated all those years ago? Remember this was an age when children were told to be seen and not heard, youngsters were instructed to stay silent at meal tables, and James Dean had not yet imported the emerging power of the teenager into UK culture. Everyone was meant to know their place.

I cannot remember his real first name. Of course, we always referred to him as 'sir' to his face. Never 'Jerry'; not even when he was well gone from the office. I think there was an unspoken fear among all of us that if the word ever left our lips in his absence, it might somehow during an unthinking moment slip out in his presence. This could only have produced sure and swift retribution of a kind unimaginable.

He spent most of his working time in his office. He had to type his own letters even though Heather was perfectly capable. He hated it, but it was in the rules that this task could not be delegated. We could hear him furiously hitting the typewriter keys, behind his closed door, as a way of venting his pent up emotions. All letters sent out had to be double-checked by the head clerk, but woe betide John B if he found anything wrong. Letters were produced in triplicate using carbon papers and mistakes could only be rectified by tearing up the originals and starting all over again.

We only had three products. Of course, they weren't called products. With such a small number, they didn't warrant a generic name. We had current accounts, seven day deposit accounts and overdrafts. Mortgages were left to building societies ("different shape balance sheet" the manager once pontificated as one of his rare contributions to my banking education) and medium term loans to corporates were a world away.

The manager was the only person allowed to lend. He enjoyed this part of his role immensely. Sometimes he would come out fully puffed up like a peacock and radiant with power.

"Just turned John Doe down flat. Wanted £75 to visit his dying mother in Australia. What does he think banks are here for?"

"Lent £50 to Fred Brown at the Post Office to rebuild his home after the gale. Told him not to tell his colleagues however. Don't want any more of these postal types coming around for money."

The word 'marketing' was never heard in banking until many years later. It would have been treated by all and sundry with much scorn and derision. I have been told that the term was first used in a banking journal in the UK when I wrote articles on American banking practices following my twelve months in the USA in the late 1960s. I remember telling a non-banking friend about what I had heard and seen during my year's scholarship across the pond and I can still remember clearly his reaction when I recounted the tales of their marketing departments:

"What nonsense. Banks don't need marketing departments. They're not selling soap flakes!"

He took control of the customer charging process at the half year. We did this as a twosome: I had to write down whatever he called out and subsequently charge it to the customer's account. It was an art not a science; there were few formal guidelines.

"Two guineas a page, one guinea extra because his credits contain so much cash, and another ½ guinea because he beat me on the golf course."

"Harrumph." He had a way of wobbling his cheeks so that the whole room quivered. "Don't like this chap. Wears brown shoes with a blue suit. Wish we could get him over to Lloyds. Call it ten guineas and let's hope he transfers."

He was the only man I have encountered before or since who lived permanently in a hotel. Well you may not have called it a hotel, but it was to me. The Royal Oak, North Street, Pewsey. It's still there; I've just looked it up on the web. He never ever let slip any personal details, but a few snippets emerged from the woodwork as they do. He was divorced and disappeared to the Isle of Wight most weekends where he was rumoured to have a long-standing relationship with a lady friend. She never put in an appearance at the branch, much as we hoped she would. He came into the office at 10am when we opened our doors to customers and left at 3pm when we closed. He took a day off each week to play golf with 'customers'. Bowls accounted for two further afternoons each week. He never appeared to break sweat. I was beginning to revise my thoughts about life with D, C and O. Perhaps UK banking wasn't too bad after all?

"Better keep things shipshape. Must be due for a visit from the Inspectors soon," he bid us farewell with one afternoon.

I told my mother that evening that I had no idea what this meant but it sounded life threatening.

"Have some more pheasant and bread sauce," she replied. It was a crime to leave food. Nothing was wasted. Any leftovers appeared in soup or bubble-and-squeak the next day. "Wash day tomorrow. Anything need doing?" she asked.

My mother did all the laundry once a week in an outside hut where clothes were boiled in water in a concrete vat, heated underneath by a coal or wood fire. There was a mangle for drying, and irons were heated on the black range in the kitchen, which was never allowed to go out. This also provided the water for baths: kettles and pans were poured into a galvanised iron tub for the once monthly full scrub. Showers we only saw in Hollywood movies on the recently acquired black-and-white television. It looked a most unsatisfactory way of getting clean.

The first television in the village saw the light of day in 1953, just in time for the Queen's coronation on the 2nd of June after the death of her father over a year earlier. It had been bought by the W's who owned the small shop in the village. They were as pleased as could be with their purchase. The set was given pride of place in their front parlour as befitted the importance of the event in Westminster Abbey and, more relevantly, their own standing in the community. The whole village was invited. The signal in Rushall was virtually nonexistent and I recall watching a white snowstorm filmed on a black starry night through a hole made in the crook of my mother's elbow. I doubt that the Queen was bothered!

"How's the brace?" asked my mother.

I had paid my second visit to the dentist before starting work and he had advised wearing a brace because, unusually, my top front teeth did not overlap my bottom set. I hated wearing it, and only put it in when my mother was watching. Not surprisingly, my teeth still don't overlap, but I can't recall anyone ever noticing in the fifty-odd years that have passed since then.

On my first visit the dentist had startled me with the innocent question: "where did you go for your holidays this year?"

My mind raced to decipher what he meant. After a few moments it came to me. I had seen it in the movies. No one in my village went on holiday. While I was at school, holidays were what happened in between terms. Farm workers had two weeks a year and spent it in their back gardens planting crops to feed their families during the twelve months ahead. Perhaps they went to the pub six nights a week

- the weekly wash -

rather than the normal four, but that was the only difference.

"Nowhere special," I replied and opened my mouth as wide as possible to prevent further attempts at obtaining clarification.

We never ate out. Why would you, when food came free and fresh from the garden or farm? The nearest restaurant was eight miles away, and you had no car and no spare money.

A year or so later, I was transferred to Barclays in Bracknell. This was before I married. I lived in digs. Shortly after my arrival, one of the other guys suggested going out for a meal. We went to a Bernie Inn – considered quite the thing in its day – and I only half knew what to do because I had read about such things in books.

"Fancy a steak?" said a couple of the other guys. "Yes," says I without having the faintest idea what it meant. At home we called beef, 'beef', not 'steak'.

"How do we want them done?" continued one of the group. Thankfully others came in first with words like 'medium' or 'rare' so I just went along with the crowd. Wasn't a patch on my mother's braised beef and freshly pulled onions, I can tell you.

A few years on, during my year in America, where I was treated like royalty by every host bank I visited, Gerry W of the Northern Trust Bank, Chicago (who became a lifelong friend), took me to my first American football game.

After the match he enquired, "Fancy a pizza?" I had never heard the word before and had not the foggiest notion whether it was animal, vegetable or mineral.

I enlisted my by now tried-and-trusted technique. "Absolutely," I replied with more nonchalance than I felt.

The pizza joint was just around the corner so at least I found out quickly it was a kind of food. I also saw how the word was spelt. "Petesah" I tried to remind myself frequently.

"What do you want on yours, Mike my buddy?" Gerry asked.

We had already started to become pals.

"Whatever you're having, mate," I quickly responded. "When in America..."

English food is often maligned. And it is true that my mother's cooking relied almost solely on locally sourced fresh produce, prepared in the pot or oven without complications, and containing little or no added spices or flavourings apart from a sprinkling of salt and pepper. Her salt came from a large block the size of a cake which somehow seemed to last forever.

But I can tell you: everything tasted the way nature intended. Meat melted in the mouth like butter. Runner beans freshly picked and sliced, broad beans still glowing from that lovely furry stuff inside their pods, brussel sprouts still kissed with last night's frost. Wonderful! I can taste it all now.

British cuisine changed over the years, with supermarkets appearing all over the place, Chinese and Indian restaurants springing up everywhere, and traditional pubs moving away from the only menu items being a packet of 'ready salted' and a pickled egg, to coq au vin or beef stroganoff to name but two dishes on a recent menu of what was then our local, The Charlton Cat.

But my mother's tastes never changed. In later life I would drive back down to Wiltshire and take her out for Sunday lunch somewhere.

"Don't want any of that foreign muck, mind," she used to instruct in a kindlier way than the words may suggest when committed to paper. "Don't like my food messed about. Can't taste nothing that way," she continued. And she was right.

Almost uniquely, Rushall had no pub. The Charlton Cat was on the edge of the nearest village rejoicing in the much lovelier name of Charlton St Peter. The establishment had originally been called the Red Lion, but an ill-painted original sign was dubbed 'the cat' by locals. The name was formally adopted in 1921.

It was a short walk away across the fields and was run with an iron hand inside a velvet glove by two sisters. We under-age lads had to enter through the rear door and were allowed to drink a little beer or scrumpy in a back room. The sisters kept a matronly eye on us to make sure we were both behaving and having a good time. Our dads were almost certainly in the adjoining bar and we were future proper customers after all.

There was a small lounge for toffs and ladies, and a public bar for the working man. In all the years I went to the pub with my stepfather, before and after leaving home, I could never entice him into the lounge bar.

"That's not for the likes of us," he would protest. "Anyway, they charge more in there."

All the proletariat were paid in cash those days, often giving their wage packets unopened to their spouses, who in return would give them their beer money for the week. In most homes, the lady of the house controlled the family finances lest excesses on cigarettes, alcohol and the odd flutter on the gee-gees would leave little left over for food and other necessities.

Which brings me back to my first branch manager, the French word 'troc', and a local ordinance passed in a market town in East Anglia in the fifteenth century.

Let's get rid of the French bit first. 'Troc' translates as banker, exchange or swap, which is what British employers over many centuries used to impose on their workers. The word became corrupted to 'truck' when anglicised, and many masters forced truck systems on their employees involving the payment of wages wholly or partly in kind. Methods varied – some were quite complicated such as renting out frames to hosiery workers and deducting a rental before earnings were passed across – but most involved the payment of tokens which could only be exchanged in the company shop using valuations set by the owner. Many attempts were made over the years to correct the worst injustices produced by these systems – the first recorded in 1411 when a local law required Colchester weavers to be paid in gold and silver rather than in merchandise or victuals – but it wasn't until the more enlightened days of the nineteenth century that serious attempts were made to enact legislation to outlaw the practices entirely.

The various protecting laws were known as the Truck Acts and they were generally successful in outlawing the more extreme and insidious practices of the past. However, as with many honest endeavours from lawmakers, they had unforeseen consequences which only came to prominence in the twentieth century and prompted them to be repealed. Workers could only be paid in 'current coin of the realm'. They had to receive cash; so no banking accounts for them then.

An attempt was made to correct matters in the 1960 Payment of Wages Act permitting payment in postal orders, cheques or direct bank credit in place of cash. However, it had several flaws and allowed a number of exclusions, so it was followed in the 1980s by a more fulsome Truck Acts Repeal Bill. In moving this Bill in the House of Lords in March 1983, Lord Harris of High Cross said:

"The origins of the Truck Acts take us back to a vanished world peopled by such ghosts as the bagmen, the petty toggers, the butties and other middlemen who paid workers in goods or in tommy tickets that could be exchanged only at the company store or truck shop which belonged to their employer."

He went on:

"Our substantive aim is to remove an obsolete barrier to spreading payment of wages by a variety of more modern, economic and safe methods than by carting £1,000 million of notes and coin around the country every pay day".

Wonderful, stirring words, but sadly lacking in commercial realism, as I was to discover first hand in the early 1990s, when I was promoted specifically to address the savage cost imbalance created in the bank by these millions of workers using their recently opened accounts as they had previously used their Friday pay packets. No matter what the merits of the laws might have been, to run such accounts at anything other than a substantial loss required internal change never before encountered. As an example, this mammoth re-engineering process included the establishment of many call centres with thousands of staff in faraway places, often with strange-sounding names, pretending they could still act like a bank manager of old from the programmed information they had about you on the screens in front of them. At least it gave birth to that marvellous line from the hit TV series *Little Britain*: "the computer says no!"

Jerry Philpott had no such issues in the 1950s of course. No computers, and the Truck Acts were still mercifully in place. And no call centres: if you phoned or wrote to the manager at Pewsey Branch, then that's who you got. And he would almost certainly know something about you. Yes, he worked short hours by today's standards, but he handled all the mail, called the ledgers back every day with the office junior and looked quickly through the day's work for unusual or interesting transactions.

His hotel was just a couple of hundred yards away from the branch (many managers in those days lived in bank-owned flats above the premises), he was well known and respected in the locality, and he kept his ear to the ground. Loans could be made or lost around the bar of The Royal Oak or at the nineteenth hole of the local golf course.

In the office he would huff and puff and snort and harrumph, but just like Captain Mainwaring he would lead the charge out of the trenches himself if he thought our reputation demanded it or our customers deserved it. He took any criticism personally and would never scold staff in front of customers. An earful might await the offending employee later, however.

He would often make decisions on his own initiative – which is a polite way of saying he exceeded his discretion – but only ever in what he considered to be the bank's and the customer's best interests. Our local district office was not always amused.

He proudly described himself as a "servant of the bank". Such description was entirely valid. He was pompous and vain, but unswervingly loyal and completely devoted to Barclays.

To truck or not to truck? I leave it to you to decide.

Chapter 6: It's not my fault

I had been at Pewsey branch around four months. There was no convenient car parking, so I continued to ride my bike each day unless it was really raining cats and dogs. I recall it was shortly after Christmas, because a few days previously I had repeated the tradition of going up to the M's house as they were finishing their Christmas lunch to pull crackers with all the guests around the table.

Before she re-married, my mother had been in service with one of the rich families in the village – the M's. She didn't live in, but cycled over from our tiny cottage with me firmly wedged in a home-made basket perched high over the rear wheel. This is one of my earliest memories, so I guess I was probably about five when the custom started. Basically, my mother was chief cook and bottle washer for this wealthy family and Christmas was an extremely busy time for her, as the M's had many guests for the festive season. My place was to sit quietly in the kitchen – being seen but not heard – until the coffee and port were being served upstairs, when I was summoned to the big and lavishly decorated dining room to pull a cracker with each of the guests. I felt like Tiny Tim. But the M's were nice, gentle people and the recollections of occasions in their big house bring back nothing but warm glows. This charitable demeanour did not stop me in later years leading parties of lads over their walled garden on scrumping expeditions – they grew marvellous blackcurrants, I recall.

I arrived that day at the branch around my normal time of 8.50am and was surprised to see John B pacing nervously outside pretending to be enjoying a cigarette.

When I was young everyone smoked. I cannot recall anyone in the village who did not. Your parents, the headmaster, the vicar – they were all constantly puffing away indoors and out. One village pal swears that he was examined by a puffing doctor with cigarette ash drifting down on him like second-hand confetti. Movie stars glamorised their posing styles with little white sticks in their hands. Newspapers were full of beguiling messages. They were cheap. There were no publicised health hazards. A packet in your pocket made you a man. Handing your fags around was both a social pleasure and an obligation. There are some mind-blowing advertisements from that period. One proudly states "more doctors smoke Camels than any other cigarette." Another shows a youthful Ronald Reagan addressing large packs of cigarettes under a brightly decorated tree: "I'm sending Chesterfields to all my friends; that's the merriest Christmas any smoker can have," he smilingly proclaims. No wonder it took me decades to kick the habit!

"Got the narks in," John B blurted. "Park your bike quickly and we'll go in together."

"I'll fill you in later," he continued, "but in the meantime, don't say a word to them. If they ask you anything, just say you're new."

I had never seen him so agitated. He was normally the epitome of Mr Suave and Urbane, especially to my eyes at the time. He was certainly the only person at the branch who could begin to handle the manager. We were, for example, always desperate for Jerry to take days and afternoons off so that we could use the mechanical adding machine and get away early. John B's technique for achieving this was to glance boldly out of the window and say something along the lines of:

"Looks like rain soon. Don't suppose you'll be playing golf today, sir."

As predictably as a head cold in spring, Jerry would bark back: "Rain, tosh! It's only water! It's what the lions drink! Trouble with you youngsters these days is that you've got no stamina."

With that, he would storm back into his inner sanctum and make a phone call to his golfing buddies encouraging them to join him on the course that day.

I followed John through the front door and into the narrow hallway, which served as our customer space. I kept my eyes down until we continued through the security door to the area reserved for staff and into the back office. I noticed John made sure that he was fully visible to Heather before she allowed him access into the secure area. The rulebook had suddenly become our bible, where every commandment was to be strictly obeyed. I could tell already that the next two weeks were not going to be a load of laughs. There were so many of them and so few of us; I knew how General Custer must have felt.

"B," growled a voice using the head clerk's surname. "I've told the lads you're in charge of getting us everything we need. You can start by booking all eight of us into The Royal Oak for a week. If it's good enough for old Philpott..."

At that time, bank inspectors and their teams had total power. They arrived unannounced. They could ask any question, look under any stone, demand any documentation. They had the power to make or break careers. They were gods.

I braved a glance up. Apart from the old growler, they all looked virtually identical: under thirty-five, fresh-faced, clean-cut, barbered so the first layers of skin had been removed, regulation black suits and spotless white shirts, keen to eat anyone and anything that got in their way. None of them smiled. Fraternisation with the guilty-until-proven-innocent was clearly not allowed. They were the untouchables.

Getting on Inspection was considered a good career move. You got a special allowance and were able to claim all travelling and hotel expenses; a distant dream for most branch-based clerks. Impress your bosses and a foot on the first step of a very long managerial ladder awaited you. And if you're a member of the Stazi the way not to impress your boss is to report that "everything's fine and we could find not a single irregularity."

Their first immediate task was to check all our liquid assets. That's not alcohol, silly, not a drop of that was allowed on the premises. All keys were relinquished to them straightaway and off they raced checking the cash, foreign currency, travellers' cheques, bearer bonds and open securities. Put bluntly, anything which any of us might have run off with and converted into quick readies to enjoy the Rio sunshine.

Someone had to watch them while they were in the strong room, just in case they themselves were later accused of some heinous crime (this delicious thought came to our minds quite often during that fortnight).

"Stand just there," said Growler. Luckily he didn't know my name yet.

"Lots of coin bags here."

"Yes sir," I spluttered. "We are bankers to Pewsey Carnival and collect a lot of coin from a charity well they place in the river."

"Mainly copper by the look of it, lads. No need to open them all, just kick the bags and make sure they're not full of sand." Did he break into the glimmer of a smile as he said this?

Immediately, a young member of his team hammered a finely polished shoe into a tightly packed canvas coin-bag.

Clouds of river dust swirled out and upwards. No one spoke.

Clean shoes coughed.

Pewsey Carnival was the event of the year for us village lads. There was nothing else like it in our galaxy. People travelled many miles to join in what the organisers described as 'The Best in the West'. It's still going strong after more than one hundred years.

Everything we could imagine and a few things we couldn't were going on. Real speedway racing in one of the meadows; the smell of scorched grass; the unique taste of burnt high octane fuel; the whine of protesting engines - what a heady mixture.

A proper, fully equipped funfair. Dodgems, the big wheel, candyfloss, shooting galleries – why did this only happen once a year? Best of all for us was the tattooed lady tent. Banned by our parents, which meant the queue of hot-blooded teenage males was the longest of any stall. For fourpence you could see as much female flesh in fifteen minutes as you were likely to set eyes on for the whole of the rest of the year combined. A couple of months ago, I went to a Barry Cryer one-man show in Guernsey. It all came flooding back to me when he joked:

"We used to pay to see the fat, tattooed lady. Now every high street is full of them, and it's for free!"

Bowling for the pig was one of the high spots of the week and was taken especially seriously. Like most great games invented by the British, this was later pinched by the Yanks and emasculated into an indoor game only fit for girls and babes in arms. Three wooden balls were rolled briskly along a wood plank alley to nine wooden pins in a diamond configuration surrounded by bales of straw to stop the missiles once they had passed their targets. Only men participated. They would often pay for many turns during the week after checking the winning score and top name at any particular point. Winning came with vast bragging rights. Not only would a pig feed your whole family for a year and enable you to flash a certain amount of "now every high street is full of them"

FUN FAIR
THE

generosity around the village, but more importantly people would talk about you in hushed terms of reverence: "he done got the pig at Pewsey, you know".

The culmination of the event on the Saturday evening was magic. It started after dark. Thousands of fairy lights – each one a small coloured glass jar with a lighted candle inside – illuminated the procession route like an avenue of stars. I was in the Rushall & Charlton Prize Silver Band along with my two best friends. We led the parade, so even though I could barely play a note correctly, there was some reflected glory to be had. The uniform didn't do any harm at the fairground afterwards either.

My lack of musical prowess was well known to the bandleader, so I normally marched alongside the big drum, where my squeaky outpourings could be well hidden. This was a large, heavy brute of an instrument, which was carried and played by Big Dave, a young and heavily muscled labourer from the farm. Using two large-headed sticks, he would belt the skins as if his very life depended on it.

And one year, it nearly did. We had marched in the procession for about a mile. The noise was deafening, the twinkling candles provided the only light, the pavements were so packed that the crowds were spilling on to the streets and suddenly Dave and I sensed a shape coming towards us out of the blackness from the roadside. It was a youth of around seventeen, clearly the worse for wear, with a long-bladed flick-knife thrust forward. He was after the drum, our drummer, or both. Suddenly, before I had fully taken the scene in, Dave had swung one of his mallets, catching his assailant a mighty blow just behind the ear. The attacker fell like a stone, we stepped over him and marched on.

Ted H, our conductor, who never lost an opportunity to tell us he had been to the Royal Military School of Music at the famous Kneller Hall, had seen nothing of the incident and shouted from the front using his clipped, ex-army voice:

"Come on Dave, no slacking. Keep up the beat, man, keep up the beat." Dave smiled. He knew he had entered the folklore of the band that night. And so he had. People are still telling his tale, aren't they?

"OK lads, get on with it. Got to take the ledgers out before lunch," Growler demanded. The bank inspection continued.

I shivered in the cold, dark strong room. The ledgers were my responsibility and I felt a heavy cloud of guilt descending on me, even though I didn't know enough about possible frauds to be anything other than completely innocent.

The Growler's name was Gotobed. Honestly, it was. I have never met anyone before or since with that surname. I had no idea how to pronounce it, so for once I was pleased that I could hide behind 'sir'. He was shorter and stouter than Jerry, but apart from that they shared similar genes. Growler never walked, he stomped. He never asked, he demanded. He made sounds that were more wild animal than human.

His reputation travelled well before him around the district. While he might pull the odd wing or two off little butterflies such as me, his real delight apparently was bringing branch managers to their knees.

A favourite fraud then and now was to open fictitious loan accounts, pocket the amount supposedly lent, and dribble back in repayments a little over time to allay suspicion. It was often difficult to spot this internally concocted crime, but the Growler had recently caught and sacked a manager who had been using his ill-gotten gains obtained in this way to finance a lady he had on the side. He was best known in the district for his other love: cricket.

According to the grapevine, when asked how he had uncovered the fraud, the Growler was reputed to have said:

"Middle stump trouble, old boy. Middle stump trouble. I can always spot it."

No wonder Jerry was looking a tad apprehensive as he busied himself around the office pretending to undertake a few minor tasks that he wouldn't normally touch and knew precious little about.

Like hyenas marking their territory, the narks (as they were known behind their backs) only ever used green ink. All ticks were green. All initials were green. Green was good: it meant everything was OK, at least until the next item fell under their stern gaze. No one else in the whole bank, not even the chairman, was allowed to use green ink, I was told. Green became my lifetime least favourite colour.

One thing I did acquire from them, however, I retain to this day. There was an enormous amount of initialling to be done. Everything could be traced back to its source. At school I never had cause to initial anything, so at the branch it took me about ten times longer than anyone else to complete this simple act. But I've always been a quick learner. I watched the inspectors. They initialled in microseconds and with great panache. So, I changed my initial. Next time you meet me, ask to see it. It's impressive and faster than a speeding bullet.

One obligatory chore for visiting inspectors was to write an appraisal report on each member of staff. Just like any other staff report in those days, this was a secret assessment. The results were never seen by or discussed with the individual concerned. The Growler undertook this task himself, partly it was assumed because he considered himself the world's greatest inquisitor where human flaws were concerned. He called in each member of staff separately to the manager's office which he had commandeered for most of the two weeks, much to Jerry's silent chagrin.

I was not asked to sit. He sat upright in the manager's chair. He shuffled papers. He opened a drawer. He had not yet looked up. The silence seemed interminable.

"Like sport, Pitcher?"

"Yes sir," and as an afterthought, "very much."

"Bank likes their young chaps to be keen on sport."

"OK, moneywise?" he continued after a pause.

"Absolutely, sir." Even I could work that ploy out.

"How are you finding it here?" his tone left no room for any other answer.

"Really enjoying it, sir," I lied.

"Courting?" With this, he looked up and bored into my eyes.

"Nothing serious, sir," I somehow managed in return.

"Well good luck, my boy. Good luck."

He said these last words like a priest intoning the final rites to a prisoner on the gallows. His eyes went down, he picked up a fresh sheet from the next pile. I went out the door backwards.

"If Charon ever needs a deputy….," I thought.

"Mum, I want to go on Inspection," I confided when I got home that day.

"Didn't think you liked the police," she said absently. My mother had always harboured great ambitions for me, and was ridiculously proud of the fact that I was working for a bank.

Roughly fifteen years later when I became a real-life bank manager of a large branch in the City… well, I need hardly tell you her reaction. Her bragging rights increased exponentially.

I got promoted many times afterwards, but often had strange-sounding titles like chief operating officer. I'm sure she thought I was being handed a series of demotions. Forever afterwards, regardless of my title of the day, whenever her friends were around she would say:

"Michael's a bank manager, you know." (She never, ever, used the shortened version of my first name even when I was a toddler, so she certainly wasn't going to start now.)

By the way, I never did go on Inspection. Winning my American scholarship saved me. But my initials still look great!

And as a final twist, many years later in the early 1980s, I was asked to set up and run the first unit ever formed in the bank aimed at cutting out inefficiencies and reducing costs. My first target was the Inspection Department; it felt like a delicious turning of the tables, I have to admit. Having been untouchable for so long, cost-saving opportunities hung like ripe fruit on low branches. We saved millions of pounds by abolishing many of their ingrained customs ... including (against considerable internal resistance) the need for those individual staff reports. My boss of the day told me I should have retired immediately on the back of this unrepeatable triumph; I must admit there were few sweeter moments.

Chapter 7: Soft place in my heart

Knowing how easily I get bored, people often ask me what on earth I found to do growing up in a tiny hollow in the lovely Vale of Pewsey.

"The whole of human life was there," I say, "and you didn't have to travel anywhere to see it. It was right in front of your eyes." It has a truly soft place in my heart.

We had a church, a chapel, a little village shop, a tramp, a blacksmith, a witch, a shepherd, a thatcher, a dragon lady, ten proper soldiers, a sylvan river, some stocks (they're still there), a whore (I don't think she is), Stonehenge druids, real bullets and tanks and a back yard running to thousands of acres. Surprisingly, as I have said, the place lacked a pub. But over the fields, the Charlton Cat was purring a welcome just ten minutes walk away.

Let's get the whore out of the way first of all, shall we? I had only a sketchy understanding of what that word entailed, but that's what the ladies of the village called her. My mother, who never lost her Scottish accent, pronounced the word 'Whoooer' with a strong rolling of the final letter.

Her name would come up in the pub sometimes and knowing glances could be seen passing between the men's faces. Sorry, but that's all I know, I'm afraid. Honest.

The tramp, however, became almost a friend. We lads used to

spend hours and hours chatting with him. His name was Murphy and our mothers warned us not to go near him. But he lived in an isolated, dilapidated, condemned cottage full of dark nooks and shadowy crannies, which proved an irresistible lure. One day he just disappeared and shortly afterwards the cottage collapsed, with a little help from us lads or so it was rumoured. It didn't seem right to leave it there without him.

The witch, unfortunately, was the headmaster's wife. I don't mean she was just a nasty lady – we didn't know whether she was or not because we never stayed long enough to find out – but she looked like a witch, dressed from head to toe in black-cloaked garb, was never far from her one-eyed cat, and was rarely seen in daylight. At primary school we lived in dread of the headmaster saying:

"Come round and see me after class today." This was a much more powerful deterrent than the cane. His wife might open the door!

The ten soldiers were a relic of the war. The army had commandeered much of Wiltshire for training purposes, and you could wake up one morning and find a few young chaps in khaki literally entrenched in the bottom of your garden. We loved it. They had real guns and real ammunition. They laughed a lot because they faced no enemy in Rushall. They would give you sixpence to run errands for them. Later generations of lads might have had their Action Man dolls-for-boys, but we had the real thing.

The shepherd also became a friend, at least during the spring when he spent twenty four hours a day, seven days a week in a hut on the hills tending heavily pregnant ewes and their newborn lambs. At this time of year we would spend long contented hours with him and his charges. We became quite good at forecasting when the ewes were ready to drop their babies and we would be allowed to help with the simpler tasks like hand feeding some of the youngest, tottering lambs who for various reasons had been rejected by their mothers.

I say a friend during the spring, because his character changed completely for the nine months of the year he spent down from the hills living in the village. The kind, warm, caring man we knew in the hilltop hut didn't really seem to want to know us outside of the lambing season. Indeed, he hardly spoke to anyone and rarely joined in the various village activities.

"It's people," my mother confided one day. "He prefers sheep."

The dragon lady was also a witch, but this time in the true battleaxe sense. Interestingly, she ran a clandestine shop in her front room, which only opened on Sundays, when other shops were closed. It was mainly for emergency essentials such as cigarettes. She had a thing about bags.

I lived in dread of my stepfather saying:

"Pop down to old B's and get me twenty Woodbines. There's a good lad."

"I need to take a bag, Dad." I almost whispered, knowing that the answer would be as always that we had none.

"Where's yer bag?" Dragon B roared as I stuttered out my Dad's request in her dark, cold, smelly front room. Old B smelt just as bad.

As Laurie Lee points out in *Cider with Rosie*, country people in those days had their own individual smell. Perfumes and the like were expensive and reserved by the ladies for special occasions if they bothered at all. The equivalent for men were non-existent.

My step-aunt Ivy, who spent most of her time stooped over the constantly heated, black kitchen range of her gingerbread cottage preparing meals for her two lifelong bachelor brothers, could be recognised instantly with closed eyes. She smelt of sugar and spice and all things nice associated with fresh home-cooking. When the first male deodorants eventually reached the hidden troughs of the Salisbury Plain – my own initial experiment was with an American import called Old Spice which smelt like slowly rotting hay – we lads dabbed it on sparingly with some considerable trepidation. First, we wondered if the girls would get the wrong idea about us and secondly, it was rumoured that young army recruits from the North, likely to be encountered in the public bars of Devizes, would take one whiff of the scent as the perfect excuse to poke a clenched fist into the face of any soft bellied Southerner from whom it appeared to be radiating.

Old B smelt of stale cabbage and unwashed clothes. No perfume or deodorant would ever grace her toilette.

"Where's yer bag?" she repeated in a voice fierce enough to send the rooks fleeing from the tops of the nearby elm trees. The elms all died a few years later. People blamed a Dutch disease, but I think Old B had a hand in it. One look at my face and she knew the answer. She would yank open a large drawer of her enormous wooden sideboard with a crash. It was stuffed full of hundreds of empty paper bags.

"No-one ever brings a bag!" she thundered, ripping one out and throwing it in my direction.

Many years later, we introduced a system of mystery shoppers into Barclays UK network to check anonymously on our service standards. I wished I could have sent one back to Old B!

Was there anything we didn't have? I can think of only three.

First, there was no central heating in the cottages. Who could possibly expect a technique invented by the Romans to travel so quickly to darkest Wiltshire?

On 'brass monkey' winter evenings we would huddle around the never-allowed-to-go-out kitchen range until bedtime. To say that we rose with the sun and slept when it fell would be a slight exaggeration, but when Siberia kindly sent us their minus whatever icy offloads we weren't far away from it.

The fire door would be kept open on the coldest of nights. We sat so close it burnt our cheeks and knees bright scarlet. We made toast using long forks forged by the local blacksmith. The bread was homemade and each slice was cut at least one inch thick: real doorsteps these, none of your modern copies. Our carving knife had been re-sharpened so many times over the years that it was reduced to a third of its original width, but boy, you could shave with it.

Plastic hadn't been invented – well if it had, it hadn't reached Rushall – and local butter came in great dollops from earthenware pots, which we spread on the piping hot toast as if we were sculpting the mountains of the moon. Streamlets of melting goo would run down our chins. Amber nectar Wiltshire style! Who needed caviar and champagne?

Some years later as I was 'going up in the world' we bought a toaster. My mother couldn't believe it and refused to use it. She could barely hide a rare bout of disappointment in her only son. But the moment she lost all hope for young marrieds came when she realised that the latest generation were starting to pay extra to have their bread sliced for them. I rarely saw her speechless, but this came close. "More money than sense," she would grumble with a scowl. "Remember Belgium," she would add.

Another regular winter staple was bread and dripping. Lard was collected from the bottom of the baking tray after Sunday roast and spread thickly over the mandatory doorsteps. It was marbled with bits of meat and chocolate-brown fat.

"This'll line yer stomach fur the day," my mother promised as she scraped salt liberally over the top of this coronary-inducing feast.

Bedtime on dark nights was a hurried affair. Often I brought my “where’s yer bag?”

flannelette pyjamas down to change in the cauldron of the kitchen. Then a race upstairs to bury myself in the bedclothes before the furnace heat of the range had completely evaporated from my bones. If I changed in the bedroom, all the layers came off in one swooping motion. I failed to freeze to death in bed because of the many layers of blankets. Yes, I know modern trekking and mountaineering magazines would have you believe that 'layering' is a recent invention, but I could have slept soundly at Everest base camp with the tons of wool coverings surrounding my body as moondreams descended.

In those days people kept warm by wearing more clothes. Simple, isn't it? Nowadays people wander around houses, shops and bars in the depth of winter wearing little more than a postage stamp covering their essentials complaining that the heating is not turned up enough. No wonder our planet is crying out in despair.

My mother invented layering. OK, perhaps not invented, but she certainly promoted its cause with religious zeal. Right up to her death in her late 80s she would demand to know:

"Are ye wearin' yer vest today, Michael?" Often this question – it was really more of a command – would be shouted across a crowded room or bar. She would have made a good Speaker for the House of Commons:

"Are ye wearin' yer vest today, Prime Minister?"

Of course, had he not been, he would have been banished from the Chamber for life. But if he had possessed a modicum of common sense – an unlikely attribute among today's politicians – he would have replied in the affirmative. This is how I continued to respond over the years, even though I gave up the vest lark as soon as I left home, mortified that none of the male movie stars seemed to have taken lessons at my mother's school of fashion.

Years later I lived and worked in Los Angeles for a while. An oceanfront apartment in Santa Monica overlooking 'Baywatch' beach meant some of the raking had paid off. I brought my mother over for several visits. I noticed she never asked any of the locals if they were wearing their vests. It didn't stop her continuing to admonish me, however.

Oh, and no central heating at the village school either of course. After all, suffering is meant to be good for the soul and it was a Church of England establishment. The main classroom holding around sixty shivering pupils had one large, circular, cast-iron, coal-fired boiler. It threw out a volcanic blast over a radius of around three feet. Don't ask me to explain the physics, but outside this hidden perimeter another ice age took hold. Pupils at the nether regions of the room had icicles growing from their hats and gloves, while those close enough to the glowing epicentre stripped down to their Speedos and bikinis (well, you know what I'm trying to say).

A pal has reminded me that the hands of those outside the core warmth from the stove became so cold that they couldn't hold their pencils. Every so often they were allowed to approach the heat source and de-frost those parts of their bodies they hadn't felt for some time. However, this was only permitted in maximum groups of six. Presumably our teachers worried that larger gatherings could become so inflamed with heat madness that uncontrollable riots would be sparked by the flames. Our equivalent of a Rushall Church of England Spring? You can see the headlines:

"Rushall School stove revolution sparks countrywide uprisings. Government authorises national emergency. Education Secretary declares freezing builds healthy minds and bodies."

Secondly, the seaside was a rare and infrequent treat. We youngsters all learnt to swim in the local river. There were no adults around to coach or fuss, and cows drinking and cooling down upstream added further nutrients to the already fecund water. One of my pals used to wear two swimming costumes so that he could startle the girls by taking one pair off while standing neck deep in water and waving them around his head. This prank never failed to produce a crop of nervous but delighted giggles. No-one ever suffered in the slightest from these chlorine-free and manure-rich immersions: the prevailing theory that 'a few bad germs are good for you' seemed to be validated.

The only other bathing opportunities were the open-air public swimming pool in Devizes, which involved an entrance fee following a sixteen-mile round-trip bike ride, or the ocean, which was over forty miles away at its nearest point. This seemed like another country.

Charabanc excursions were organised a couple of times a year, collecting parents and their offspring from a cluster of villages to deposit them in seaside resorts such as Bournemouth and Swanage for the day. We looked forward to these trips for weeks ahead. For eight hours we were transported to a different world: there were so many people, and just look at all that female flesh on display.

I have two abiding memories of these days. First, changing on the beach in and out of bathing gear involved the most elaborate engineering techniques using all readily available construction materials such as deck chairs, towels and beach spades.

"Och, there's no-one watching ye lads," my mother would say after we had spent an hour or so finding one square yard of sand on a packed beach resembling a disturbed ants' nest. These days it's easy; who bothers to hide anything?

Secondly, if the weather had been kind we all came back as red as overcooked lobsters. The health hazards of too much sun were unknown, and anyway who could afford sun-tan lotion? Our burns were often so sore we could barely sleep for nights afterwards, and flakes of peeling skin fell like sad November leaves for days.

Sometimes it came off in strips and we would compete to see who could produce the longest.

Lastly, there was no multiculturalism. My dictionary's definition of this word is a "doctrine acknowledging contributions and interests of many cultures." I'm sure we would have been happy to provide such an acknowledgement if we had known any other cultures. But we didn't. Although it didn't register at the time – how could it – the village only had one culture. Its own.

During the first seventeen years of my life I only ever saw one non-white person. Once again, our parents issued warnings against us having anything to do with him and in this instance with a modicum of cause. In his early twenties he was tried and convicted of murdering his male partner. So yes, that had to be explained to us as well.

Quite a number of years later, some time after I had left home, I had brought my mother up to Berkshire for the weekend and I needed to buy something in Slough. It was her first visit to the town. We were striding along the high street when my mother exclaimed in a loud voice:

"What are all these black people doing here?"

It was not a racist remark, but a genuine enquiry. She had never seen so many non-white people before. I think she imagined that Slough was a strange place to visit if you were holidaying from Africa.

I quickly completed the shopping and hurried back to the car park. It's not that I shunned the answer; it was simply that it would have led to a very long conversation.

Chapter 8: Reminiscing

Life was very self-contained growing up in Rushall. It was womb-like. Safe, cocooned, secure, structured, isolated and well nourished. We knew we were poor, but didn't for a moment feel deprived. We neither requested nor needed help from anyone else. People fed themselves, clothed themselves, made their own amusement, helped each other and fought their own battles. They asked for nothing outside their reach and expectations were unconsciously governed by an unspoken understanding of what was possible. Life changed little from one year to another, one decade to the next.

The services of the local council in Pewsey – let alone the national government in Westminster – were barely needed or raised in conversation. No one went on the dole or sought welfare; any problems or difficulties were resolved locally.

"Just got to get on with it," was a phrase you heard all the time in those days. "Nobody owes us a living."

Looking back, this was what probably produced my lifelong distrust of big governments. Politicians and civil servants are lousy decision-makers. They waste oceanfuls of money. Their prime concern is their own survival in what are mainly well-paid, extravagantly pensioned and largely unnecessary roles. The examples are legion – as I write these words the BBC headlines refer to public anger in Cyprus over demands that all bank customers pay a one-off levy on their balances. What faceless wonders in Brussels dreamt that one up? My Granny could have told you that such a plan would be unfair, unworkable, unenforceable and doomed to failure. (The first proposals, which probably took armies of highly paid office workers months to perfect, were canned within hours of protests starting on the streets of Nicosia).

The good people of Rushall had it right. Let people take responsibility for their own lives and communities. It'll be cheaper and better.

Bill Cosby, the American entertainer, seems to agree judging by some wise words of his which have just hit me via Facebook. At the age of 83 he says he is tired:

"I'm tired of people with a sense of entitlement, rich or poor.
I'm tired of people who don't take responsibility for their lives and actions.
I'm tired of hearing them blame the government, or discrimination or big-whatever for their problems.
I'm tired of being told that I have to spread the wealth to people who don't have my work ethic."

Any contact with the law, the church, the civil service and indeed any form of authority was to be avoided if possible. You didn't want people outside your close-knit community knowing anything about your business, and there was a nervousness about dealing with organisations you didn't really understand. But above all else, there was a sense that "under the bludgeonings of chance, my head is bloody but unbowed," to quote William Henley again. We were poor, but that didn't stop us being proud.

The formal law for us lads was the local bobby cycling around three or four local villages. We were wary of him but not terrified. We committed all sorts of minor wrongs, for which the penalty if caught was a clip around the ear and a much more serious threat to "tell your parents if I catch you doing this again." In truth, our parents were the law-makers, the boundary-setters, the judges and the wardens. More than anything else, you behaved within broadly understood bounds because you didn't want to bring them shame or grief. They had hard enough lives already.

The church was not a great factor. Very few villagers were regular churchgoers, and going to a Church of England school only meant putting up with a homily from the vicar just once a week.

In the neighbouring village of Charlton St Peter – I'll give you one guess at the name of the church, my lovely grandchildren – my step-uncle Bert was for many years the only suppliant at the regular weekly Sunday evening service. Of course no-one else was there to authenticate the story, as good journalists would say, but the word was that the vicar would spend most of the hour exchanging views on the likely football results for the coming Saturday. 'Doing the pools' was all the rage in the 1950s and there was clearly nothing in the good book to forbid church members from participating along with everyone else. In 1957 a Stockport lady had won the mind-blowing sum of over £200,000 by correctly forecasting eight draws, and for a while everyone talked of what they would do with a similar amount. In those days, you could buy a decent little house in the country for less than £1,000.

I had to go to Sunday school somewhere and chose the local chapel because the songs were better, my mates went, and most of the village girls turned up in their Sunday best. I sometimes got to play my cornet which was then, as now I imagine, a good icebreaker.

Meeting girls – the word dating had not yet crossed the Atlantic – and what might subsequently follow was a pretty haphazard and very unsophisticated affair. Events at the village hall provided the main initial point of contact. Most Saturday nights, evenings would be organised for us youngsters and they would normally end with games that facilitated a modest amount of physical contact; musical chairs, blind man's buff, postman's knock and so on.

Chat-up lines were beyond our ken, so there was normally a quick and direct approach if you wanted to see the girl again as a twosome.

"Meet you behind Wookey's barn tomorrow evening around seven?" was about as romantic as it got.

As and when the encounter took place, there was little conversation, a lot of snogging, as much groping as you could get away with (we lads gave numbers to the various stages, so rather than waste words on lurid details, you simply reported to your chums the following day that you had got to stage three or whatever), but very little (if any) full sex. The pill had not yet been invented, and the fear of having an unwanted baby at that stage of life was a powerful contraceptive for both boy and girl. My parents would have been mortified: "Fancy throwing away all that reading and education, Michael". I can hear my mother saying it. Most people waited until they got married. Indeed, lust was a strong incentive to wed early.

Our relationship with our parents was both close and distant. The cottage was always there in the background with warmth, the smells of the kitchen, the unchanging decoration, the eternal sanctuary. But outside the front door we were away doing what we wanted with no adult supervision. Swimming in the river, climbing trees, thrashing around the barns, hanging around the village shop, scrambling over the hayricks, playing pretend soldiers in the target tanks on the boundary of Salisbury Plain, fighting in the fields with mud clods left over from harvested cornfields, building straw-bale houses, helping the blacksmith as he forged horseshoes, talking to

Murphy in his abandoned house, sailing in cattle-feeding troughs down the river, popping into the local pub through the back door if we were still under age, and, of course, smoking all the time if we could raise enough money for the odd Woodbine or two.

My stepfather was a kind and simple man, who laboured on the same land as his ancestors. He came from a family of thirteen, mainly boys. Some died in childhood, the surviving girls went into service and the lads all became farm labourers. This was the normal, seemingly pre-ordained pattern. For fun, he cycled to the local pub several times a week, as did all his fellow farm workers. He never owned a car, never flew in an aeroplane, never went abroad, never had a banking account, never had a holiday in today's sense, never went sick, rarely saw a doctor or dentist.... and never complained about his lot. No different to any of his mates. He voted Labour the whole of his life and would have cut off his right arm before supporting the Tories. I often discussed this with him and I came to the view that this unwavering stance was more akin to supporting your local football club than born out of any deep sense of political conviction. I'm sure he would have detested present-day socialists, but voted for them anyway!

My mother proudly came from 'north of the border' and like many women of her generation she was tough, wiry, energetic, hard-working and a survivor. She was always on the go. All food had to be prepared from scratch. She could skin a rabbit or pluck a goose in the blinking of an eye. There were none of today's labour saving devices such as dishwashers, driers, washing machines, vacuum cleaners and so on. After she married, she worked part-time at the village school as caretaker, cleaner and dinner server (members of her son's gang were quietly given extra portions). Like most of the village ladies, she appeared not to possess or desire any time for relaxation. Evenings were spent sewing, knitting, mending, patching, darning.

- we are sailing -

We got our first TV in the late 1950s, but the spluttering, black and white picture quality was so poor we hardly watched it. When I acquired my first house after marriage, as well as being struck dumb by my back garden, my London overspill neighbours could not believe that I did not consider a TV an essential early acquisition.

The village primary school was largely designed to stop us bothering our parents and getting into more trouble for two thirds of the year. The classes were big, every afternoon was devoted to sports which involved being turned out into the very expansive grassed playground from lunch onwards. School finished at 3pm to allow children to take tea to their fathers working in the fields. Neither I nor my friends from those days can recall receiving anything resembling a proper lesson. We copied words from the blackboard and listened to constant admonishments to be quiet, and that was about it. Luckily I was able to do my reading privately.

Like most in the village, we had no books whatsoever at home. We did acquire one, however, when I was around twelve years old.

In those days the local Church of England vicar was a person of some considerable authority. The farm labourers would touch their caps as he passed by. We lads would vaguely stand to attention and call him "sir", unless we saw him coming with sufficient time to dive behind a bush first. To us he was boring, yet terrifying. He would call on all the houses from time to time, completely unannounced. As befitted his station, he always entered through the front door. Normally we only used this room for special occasions such as Christmas and funerals.

The front knocker went and there he was: "Just want to see how Michael is getting on at the grammar school," he intoned.

My mother ushered him into the front room and desperately searched for the best crockery. Once again, the best cups and saucers were normally reserved for weddings and high days.

Seeking whatever support she could get my mother called out: "Michael, the Reverend T is here and wants to have a word."

I was hiding behind the door to the kitchen trying desperately to remember which one of my several recent peccadillos might have come to his ears.

I could hide no longer. " Ah, Michael," he said with a kindlier tone than I had encountered before, "thought we might pray on the family Bible for your continuing scholastic success".

My mother's face fell, her cheeks turned puce, her lips tightened into thin, white lines, and her eyes became drained of all emotion. The silence seemed to last a lifetime.

"Oh, what a shame, vicar," she managed eventually, "I lent it to a friend just yesterday."

We acquired our first and only book a few days later after her weekly shopping trip to Devizes. She was not going to be caught out like that again! I can't recall we ever opened it.

However, courtesy of being a paperboy, I did regularly get two weekly comics: *The Rover* and *The Wizard*. They each had one or two cartoon strips but in the main they were composed of stories for reading.

I read them from cover to cover. My favourite was Wilson the Wonder Athlete. This unassuming loner – you can see the similarity emerging already – through will-power and iron discipline had learned how to slow his heart-rate right down and perform the most amazing sporting feats. He was the first man to climb Everest, he captained England to an Ashes victory in Australia, and ran the first four-minute mile (although Wilson himself protested a Yorkshireman, one Benjamin Nutsford, first achieved this feat in 1774); the list was endless.

The Wizard was my bible, and Wilson my hero. In truth, I think he was my first and last.

Also, the father of one of my closest friends, one of the few males in the locality not to work on the farm, had long been a member of a postal book club and had built up a large and varied library. I have often thought this was another slice of the large helping of good luck I have received during my life.

I devoured them. I read everything I could lay my hands on. Hemingway, Steinbeck, Huxley, Lawrence, Orwell became my friends long before I realised they were famous.

Thank you, Mr Miller. You and *The Wizard* contributed more to my education than any of us realised at the time. And, now I have several bookcases of my own, *The Truth about Wilson* by W.S.K. Webb takes pride of place.

Sports we learnt in the fields. We would fish in the sweetly flowing River Avon with cotton lines and bent pins for hooks. Sometimes we even caught a fish! Cricket skills were honed in the nearest flat meadows with a third-hand tennis ball and any old piece of wood that vaguely resembled the shape of a bat. Soccer was even easier: anything round to kick and a couple of jumpers for goal posts. Needle matches were played regularly with lads from nearby villages; these often turned a little nasty towards the end, as rival female supporters were tempted to switch their favours. More West Side Story than Wiltshire harmony!

It only occurred to me more clearly in later life, that no one actually owned anything, apart from the proverbial clothes on their back. The roof over our heads was owned by the farmer and went with the job. Clothes were homemade or secondhand or both. Your one pair of shoes had to be worn until the soles of your feet were in danger of showing through before a fresh pair could be acquired.

It was a cash- and barter-based economy in the principality of Rushall. There was no credit. No-one had a banking account. No-one had a mortgage. No-one had anything to borrow money for. If you couldn't afford it from cash in hand, then you went without. Just imagine how I have bored my children with these and similar tales over the years.

There was little if any envy, because everyone was in the same boat. And little stigma attached to us lads for the same reason. As I have said, this changed somewhat when I went to the Grammar School, where I encountered rich kids for the first time. 'Rich' meant they weren't getting free meals and other handouts like me.

But I have to tell you that I count my lucky stars that I grew up without much in the way of possessions. Everything else since has meant so much more as a consequence. And I still don't like my food 'messed about'; give me a potato baked in the flickering embers of an open fire loaded with fresh butter and cheese any day. Delicious!

Chapter 9: Heartbeat

Devizes was a mysteriously wonderful place to us village lads. Of course we had heard of cities like London and Manchester, but they were in a different solar system - untouchable, unreachable, unimaginable.

Devizes was within our grasp; we could get there by catching a bus or riding our bikes. It was daunting and exciting at one and the same time. With a population of around 10,000 in those days, it had everything.

A proper castle, an amazing canal system, thirty five pubs (one of my pals claims to this day that one evening he had a beer in each), its own brewery with working shire horses, a railway station, two cinemas, barracks housing hundreds of soldiers, white horses cut from chalk hills, the first coffee shop in the county, a courthouse and prison, and the dreadful tale of Ruth Pierce, kept alive to this day by the salutary inscription written on the market cross:

"On Thursday the 25th January 1753, Ruth Pierce of Potterne in the County, agreed with three other women to buy a sack of wheat in the market, each paying her due proportion towards the same. One of the women, in collecting the several quotas of money, discovered a deficiency and demanded of Ruth Pierce the sum which was wanting to make good the amount. Ruth Pierce protested that she had paid her share, and said that 'she wished she might drop down dead if she had not'. She rashly repeated this awful wish; when to the consternation and terror of the surrounding multitude, she instantly fell down and expired, having the money concealed in her hand."

The coroner, one John Clare, recorded that she had been "struck down dead by the vengeance of God".

Whew! Ready for a coffee after that? Join me at the Oasis Coffee Shop in the marketplace, or to give it the trendy name of the 50s: espresso bar. This was the latest rage, imported from America like most other things exciting us teenagers at the time, and Devizes had one! Our mothers absolutely forbade us to go there, so it had to be good. And it most definitely was!

Rich, frothy coffee the like of which we had never seen before, with brown sugar on the side to go with it; the first we had ever tasted. But it gets better: a new phenomenon was just reaching the youngsters of Devizes, which was beginning to frighten parents the length and breadth of the country. It was a new dress craze that for once had not been conceived across the Atlantic. It was home-grown, born in the less salubrious parts of London. It had recently prompted the chairman of Dartford Juvenile Court to be quoted as pronouncing that the garb "stamped the wearers as Nazis".

Strong stuff indeed, especially as all that was being described was young men dressed up in gear that was partly inspired by the styles worn by dandies in the Edwardian period. Long, brightly coloured frock coats with velvet collars, bootlace ties, drainpipe trousers, fluorescent socks, thick crepe soled shoes (known affectionately as brothel creepers) and a quiffed hairstyle, which must have generated enormous profits for Brylcreem in its day. On the 23rd of September 1953 a Daily Express headline shortened Edward to Teddy, coined the term 'Teddy Boy' and the description stuck. Their girls were known as Judies for some reason I have yet to fathom, typically sporting ponytails and voluminous circle skirts. We thought it looked great; unfortunately from the full gear we could only afford the glowing socks so that had to do.

Even better than any of this – wonder of wonders – they had a jukebox!

I had never seen or heard anything like it before. On my first visit, one record changed my life. Someone called Buddy Holly was singing his latest recording, 'Heartbeat'.

"Why do you miss when my baby kisses me?
Heartbeat,
Why does a love kiss stay in my memory?"

I was on fire. I went straight out and bought the record even though I would have nothing to play it on until well after I got married in 1965. In March 1958, Buddy Holly and the Crickets toured the UK and I was there to clap and stomp them with the rest of a packed and screaming audience at the Salisbury Playhouse. Less than one year later on the 3rd of February 1959 he was dead at the age of twenty-two, killed in a completely unnecessary light plane crash leaving his pregnant wife a widow after barely six months of marriage and fans the world over aghast at such a tragic loss. The day the music died was later immortalised by Don McLean in his classic 'American Pie'.

Somehow over the years I lost the programme from this spellbinding event, but I have kept the faith by being a lifelong aficionado. It wasn't until I was in my 60s that I undertook my own equivalent of the haj to Lubbock, Texas and Buddy Holly's grave. He lies alongside his mother, who maintained his bedroom unchanged and private while she lived, although it is now preserved in the Buddy Holly Museum in Lubbock for all to see.

"Shouldn't you be bowing?" said my girlfriend at the graveside.

"I'm just sharing with them this little story about my first record "why do you miss when my baby kisses me?"

OASIS COFFEE BAR

purchase," I said. "I'm sure they get the joke."

After a cup of coffee in the Oasis why not pop along to the best pastry shop the world has ever known? One step inside and you will be hooked for life: the smell of freshly baked bread, cakes and all manner of other goodies is irresistibly heavenly. It hits you like a giant wave of scent, so dense that you could swim to eternity and back in it. One intake of this blissful aroma had grown men dropping to their knees pleading to be left alone lying on the floor forever.

We are in The Pie Shop, Market Place, Devizes. It was famous across the length and breadth of the West of England. Folks were said to travel hundreds of miles for its wonderful freshly cooked delights. Cream slices, currant buns, pies, rolls – it had the lot, but its piece de resistance was the Wiltshire Lardy Cake. This unique creation deserves those capital letters for it is in a class of its own. We used to eat it hot with lashings of fresh butter and strawberry jam. Delicious! However, a word of warning to those readers who may be watching their weight; with generous helpings of butter and lard as prime ingredients, one slice probably provides more than sufficient calories for a whole week.

The 1967 film of Thomas Hardy's novel *Far from the Madding Crowd* was largely filmed in Devizes and one of the stars, Terence Stamp, would often go in to buy lardy cakes for his then girlfriend, the model Jean Shrimpton. Quite how she remained so slim on such fare is anyone's guess. During a chance encounter with one of the extras more than forty years after the filming, Mr Stamp said the shop selling the pies was the feature of the town he most remembered. He is reported as saying that everyone tried not to be the first on the set, because their job would then be to go across and queue up for all the doughnuts and pastries required by the crew that day.

The Pie Shop was also famous for its 'stales'. Everything was freshly baked on the premises and it all had to go on the day of production to be sold at regular prices. However, the following day whatever was left over was pensioned off for virtually nothing. This was the bit that we lads liked: we couldn't afford the normal prices, but for sixpence (2 ½ p in today's money), you could get a huge bag of mixed leftovers from the previous day's baking. There would be enough in one bag for half a dozen of us to feast on during both school morning and afternoon breaks and the homewards bus journey in the evening. Was that paradise, or what?

The bus trips to and from school each weekday are also worth a note or two in their own right. It was a public service on the classic British double-decker with an unspoken and voluntary rule that we schoolkids sat upstairs and sensible members of the general populace sat downstairs. This unofficial arrangement suited both: oldies had a little peace and quiet while we youngsters made enough noise on the upper deck to scare the troops on manoeuvres over the Plain. It generated its own camaraderie.

The bus started in Salisbury in the mornings and threaded its way through many small villages before decamping us in Devizes. Many of the early pick-ups for the upper deck involved the children of serving military personnel from places rejoicing in such names as Figheldean, Netheravon and East Chisenbury. One of the pupils from these early stops later became the most famous person the school produced during the period I was there. I would never have guessed it at the time and neither would many of my fellow travelling grammar school students.

She was a shy, skinny, self-conscious wisp of a thing who made no impression on us lads whatsoever. How wrong can you be?

The then Sandra Paul who first married jazz pianist Robin Douglas-Home at the age of eighteen, became a world-renowned model in the 1960s with acquaintances reportedly including Frank Sinatra and John F Kennedy. She is now Baroness Howard of Lympne, wife of Michael Howard, a former leader of the Conservative Party and is a successful novelist in her own right. Her website suggests she has grown lovelier and lovelier over the years. Did I ever share a 'stale' with her, I wonder? And would she remember if I had?

The Pie Shop was a legend and so were some of its staff. One Doris Perdue who worked at the shop for over thirty years until well into her 80s was affectionately known throughout Devizes and surroundings as Nana Pie. Sadly, neither Nana nor her long-term employers are still with us. But if these few paragraphs have left you feeling peckish, there are still places where you can enjoy a helping or two of Wiltshire lardy cake. Remember – hot with loads of butter and jam.

And where better to enjoy a few stales than one of the two cinemas. The Rex and the Regal, I think they were called. At last, somewhere to take a girl which didn't involve both parties getting wet, green, grassy bottoms or haystalks coming out of everywhere. They had special Saturday morning performances where for sixpence you got to watch both A and B movies and enjoy an ice-cream during the interval. This break lasted for around fifteen minutes and we all left our seats and raced around the picture palace like the cowboys and indians we had just been watching. It was also a good place for a snog – there were no adults, it was dark and everyone else was doing it.

In this part of Wiltshire the military presence was everywhere and had been for centuries. The army were so much a part of the backdrop that you almost forgot they were there. The rather forbidding Le Marchant Barracks, home to the Wiltshire Regiment for many years, had processed thousands of recruits over the decades and provided a steady supply of customers for the many local pubs and abundant flirting opportunities for the ladies of the town, both young and old.

The nearby chalk plateau covering three hundred square miles which is the Salisbury Plain remains the largest military training area in the UK. I didn't fully appreciate the scale of it all until I took up marathon and long-distance trail-running after my retirement, many years later. In preparation for a London Marathon, one early spring I joined a race jointly organised by the Warminster Running Club and the local Army Garrison. All finishers received a medal and a coffee mug. I'm still using the mug – the inscription on it reads "Imber Half – I found the lost village of Imber". Let me explain the background.

On the 1st of November 1943, about a year after I was born as it happens, in preparation for Operation Overlord, the one hundred and fifty inhabitants of this tiny village marooned almost in the middle of the Plain were given forty-seven days to leave their homes. The place was to be used by US troops to practise street fighting. The villagers were told they would be able to return after the war. This promise has yet to be honoured and the village remains a chilling and evocative monument. After running for around six-and-a-half miles, passing numerous signs warning of unexploded bombs and shells, suddenly the sad sight of the lost village emerges. The church remains intact although badly in need of restoration. An annual service is still held there on the Saturday nearest to St Giles Day. The pub is still recognisable with 'Bell Inn' just about decipherable from the swaying sign, but you would be the only customer and there's no beer or barmaid left. The rest of the village looks like a scene from *The Hurt Locker.* As we ran back to Warminster, most of the participants were strangely silent.

"That's as close as I've been to a war zone," said one of the other runners, "it's been raped, heart, body and soul."

The Wikipedia entry on Imber records that one Albert Nash, who had been the village blacksmith for over forty years, was found sobbing over his anvil when the forced evacuation news broke and later became the first resident to die and be brought back to St Giles Church for burial.

I'm looking at my mug again. "It's always winter in Imber," I'm thinking. It was a sad run.

Alcohol was a part of our lives from an early stage. Well, be fair, there were thirty five pubs and booze was cheap. Scrumpy – an apple cider indigenous to the West Country – was sixpence a pint in its roughest, cloudiest form. It produced horrendous hangovers and dreadful cases of the galloping trots, and so was best saved for those occasions when cash flow had dried up to a trickle, even if other outpourings hadn't!

And of course we had our own brewery, Wadworths. The best beer in the world, so my stepfather frequently used to say. He had lots of derogatory phrases about all other brands, including one in particular that he insisted took courage to drink.

Like most other scholastic establishments, the Grammar School organised field trips and educational outside visits. The annual trip to The Northgate Brewery just down the road from the school premises was the most fought over excursion of all. You were allowed to sample the beer with teachers watching!

According to their website, it was all started in 1875 by Henry Alfred Wadworth at the age of twenty-two. By then, apparently, he already had six years of brewing experience. No university degree for him then?

We took every opportunity we could to slip off to the pub. On Fridays during term time, we were allowed to stay late at the

Grammar School for dancing classes. These took place in the main hall and as it was a co-educational school, there were always lots of girls in attendance. It started around 6.30pm and finished about 9pm, just in time to allow us village yokels minutes to race to the market place and catch the last bus home. The final bus of the day meandered through every village and hamlet in Wiltshire, or so it seemed.

In spite of all the talent on show, most of us lads would disappear at 6.40pm to the nearest pub, which was a tiny place with barely room to swing a cat, called The Artichoke. The scrumpy would flow... well, like scrumpy. At 8.50pm we would rejoin the mainly female dancers for the last waltz.

"You've been drinking," my mother would say when the last bus had finally deposited me into the thatched cosiness of our little cottage.

"Just a spot of Dutch courage for the dancing," I would always reply.

But of course the main difference about Devizes for us village youths was the people. None of them seemed to work on a farm. They were accountants, solicitors, civil servants – all looking just the same in their black suits, white shirts and natty hats. All the workers in the village wore cloth caps covered in holes and grease stains. Few of them owned a suit and if any did, it only put in an appearance for funerals and weddings and would be taken off and returned to the wardrobe immediately after any such event was over.

And they all spoke differently. The branch manager at Pewsey had pointedly remarked to me at an early stage:

"Never get anywhere with that rustic accent, Pitcher," he snorted. "Bank doesn't like accents."

I didn't know at the time that I had an accent – it sounded just the same as everybody else in the village to me – but meeting a few of these Devizes folk showed me the error of my understanding.

I was never going to touch that moon speaking like a Moonraker! So a belated thank you to the snooty, but well-spoken folks of Devizes for helping me in at least one regard.

My accent still reverts when I return to the sylvan Pewsey Vale of course; otherwise some of the locals would not understand me, and my old friends would consider that I had lost all touch with my roots.

And there are still times when only the gentle burr of that part of the world will do a subject justice. As an example, it's simply impossible to sing the county song of Wiltshire using the Queen's English. Try it for yourself:

T'were on a jolly zummer's day, the twenty-fust of May,
John Scroggins took his turmut hoe, wi' thic he trudged away,
Now zome volks they loike haymakin', and zome they vancies mowin'
But of all the jobs as Oi loike best, gi'e Oi the turmut 'oein'.

Chorus:
The vly, the vly –
The vly be on the turmut,
'Tis all me eye,
Fer Oi to try,
To keep vlies off them turmuts.

The fust place as Oi went to wurk; it were wi' Varmer Gower,
Who vowed and swore as how Oi were ' - a virst class turmut 'oer';
The second place Oi went to wurk, they paid Oi by the job,
If Oi'd a-knowed a little more, Oi'd sooner a'bin in quod.

Chorus

The last place as Oi went to wurk, they zent ver Oi a-mowin',
Oi zent wurd back, Oi'd zunner get the zack, than gi'e up turmut 'oein'.
Now all you jolly varmer chaps, wot boides at 'ome zo warm,
Oi'll now conclude my ditty wi'e a-wishin' you no 'arm.

This stirring song – known both as The Vly be on the Turmot and The Turnip Hoer's Song – was adopted as the regimental march by the Wiltshire Regiment and is traditionally sung from the balcony of the White Hart Hotel, Salisbury, after each election by the winning Parliamentary candidate.

Again, try singing it without adopting some sort of rural accent. It's impossible. If you want to know the tune, there is a wonderful version on YouTube by Fred Perrier and the villagers from the community of West Lavington recorded in 1950. His words do not follow the official version, so please feel free to compose some of your own. Wiltshire is a very forgiving place.

So now, in the closing words of the song, I conclude this ditty with wishing you no harm. Keep raking, and may all your moondreams come true.

"may all your moondreams come true"

Thanks

This is not easy. Where to begin and where to end?

The desire to include all those people who have helped me along the journey in ways great and small is immense. But I might forget someone and cause unintended disappointment? Worse, I might feel obliged to mention someone who doesn't deserve it!

So let me do it this way. We are all touched by hundreds if not thousands of fellow human beings – the good, the bad, and the ugly – as we travel life's road. And they all make some contribution to our development, often in ways not fully understood or intended at the time.

So let me acknowledge with thanks and gratitude everyone who has attempted to help, guide, assist and encourage me over the years. I'm sorry if I didn't always appear grateful at the time!

A few must be named:

¤ Mill and Hank for a lifetime of unquestioned and unquestioning friendship.

¤ Buddy Holly for the music that has never died. All chapter headings are taken from his song titles.

¤ Alfred Wainwright for kindling my undying passion for the Lake District. Love letters they still are.

¤ Gilbert Lawford Dalton (aka W.S.K Webb) for so vividly creating Wilson the Wonder Athlete. No youngster could ask for a greater hero.

“It's called a crop circle,” I said.

TRICORN
BOOKS